CAPITALISM VERSUS PLANET EARTH

CAPITALISM VERSUS PLANET EARTH
An Irreconcilable Conflict

FAWZI IBRAHIM

Muswell Press Ltd

Capitalism versus Planet Earth

Text © Fawzi Ibrahim 2012

© Muswell Press Ltd 2012

First published in Great Britain 2012

ISBN 978-0-9568920-8-9

A CIP record of this book is available from the British Library

Typeset by JS Typesetting Ltd, Porthcawl, Mid Glamorgan

Cover design by Barney Beech
Printed and bound by Short Run Press

Muswell Press Ltd
www.muswell-press

In memory of
Reg Birch – a friend and comrade.

Contents

... traces the present environmental degradation
back to the Industrial Revolution, the birth of
modern-day capitalism and asks if our planet's
environmental woes are a result of human activity
in general or the existing economic system.

... outlines the theoretical underpinnings of
mainstream environmental movements such as
'natural capitalism'. This chapter argues that by

designating natural resources as capital, they
become commodities and, like other commodities,
are open to trading for profit.

... takes issue with those 'new economists'
who consider economic laws to be man made,
contrasting their approach with the scientific
analytical approach of Adam Smith, David
Ricardo and Karl Marx. This chapter explains
the basis of Marx's theory of the tendency of the
rate of profit to fall, extending it to modern-day
capitalism and introducing the concept of the
'critical zone'. Using a technique widely employed
in science and engineering, it constructs a
3-variable graph of the 'operating map of capital'
and goes on to explain how the toxic combination
of vast capital accumulation and pressure on the
rate of profit to fall inevitably leads the economy
towards a 'critical zone' in which production for
profit becomes unviable.

... challenges those who wish to bypass the
economic laws of capitalism with concepts like the
'tyranny of the bottom line' and the 'post-growth

economy', arguing that, far from being an optional extra, growth is an indispensible necessity for capitalism. It demonstrates that the 'polluter pays' principle is an excuse for passing extra costs on to the consumer, allowing the capitalist to make higher profit.

... argues that the post-2007 financial/economic crisis is not the 1930s all over again, but far worse: it is a crisis of capital deficiency as capital approaches the 'critical zone'. Contrary to popular conception, the post-2007 crisis was not caused by greedy bankers or incompetent politicians, but was a result of the inherent laws of highly advanced capitalism. In this economic quagmire, the belief that we can make capitalism constrain its behaviour for the sake of the planet is illusory.

... maintains that, far from being the natural order of things, capitalism, like all economic systems that preceded it, is a passing phase that is waiting to be superseded. The chapter looks at the 'cash-free' internal economy of the pre-reform NHS as a blueprint for a post-capitalist, non-commodity economy.

List of Figures and Tables

FIGURES

TABLE

Preface

We entered the 21st century with a widespread consensus of a potential environmental catastrophe if global temperatures were allowed to rise by more than 2°C. By the end of the first decade of the century, following the collapse of Lehman Brothers, an equally widespread consensus began to emerge. The post-2007 financial/economic crisis was no ordinary crisis; it was a crisis of a kind that the world had never experienced before. The 'old normal' of boom-and-bust cycles was replaced with the 'new normal' of a lost generation, unemployment and falling living standards.

It is puzzling that, so far, there has not been any consideration as to whether it is just a coincidence that the environment is heading towards a tipping point at the same time as capitalism faces a crisis of equally serious dimensions, or whether the two crises are related in some way. Is there cause and effect; a relationship between the crisis in global capitalism and that of the planet's environment? This book considers these questions and asks if planet Earth is safe with capitalism. Can there be a cohabitation between expansive, profit-at-any-cost capitalism and the Earth's delicately balanced ecosystem? Can capitalism be tamed, regulated, humanised, to take care of the future of the planet? Can there be harmony between Mother Nature and capitalist predatory instinct? The answer is an emphatic 'no'. In the process of this analysis, the theories that underpin what is generally referred to as the environmental movement are challenged and their solutions questioned. It isn't that some of the solutions are without merit; they are just ineffective in a capitalist system – a system that is more occupied with saving itself than saving the planet.

With the exception of the 'critical zone' theory and its associated economic operating map of capital, I do not claim originality. For this reason, comprehensive and detailed references are provided to acknowledge the sources of other ideas and theories. The concept of the 'critical zone' is a derivative of Marx's theory of the tendency of the rate of profit to fall as technology advances and capital accumulates. I arrived at the 'critical zone' theory as far back as 1970. It remained in a manuscript form, gathering dust, for 37 years. It was aired in public for the first time at a seminar with a small Marxist gathering at The Calthorpe Arms, Kings Cross, on 1 September 2007 and subsequently published in *Communist Review* (Autumn 2008).

I wish to record my thanks to the small group of Marxists that I have been associated with for a number of years and, more especially, for the exchanges that I have had with John

Haywood, Geoff Woolf, Don Kirkley and Akan Leander, usually in a pub over a pint or two of real ale, for their willing engagement, intelligent enquiry and critical encouragement, without which this work would have been the poorer. And finally a very huge 'thank you' to my wife Valerie for her consistent, unequivocal and unqualified support.

Fawzi Ibrahim
May 2012

Foreword

This book is unique and, if you care about the planet that sustains us, required reading. It is about the dangerous intersection of ecological crisis and economic crisis. Fawzi Ibrahim argues persuasively that the laws that govern capitalism make it unable to combat climate change and its life-threatening effects; that the latest economic crisis has raised the conflict between capitalism and planet Earth to a whole new level, since the very survival of the socioeconomic system is now at risk. And so we face a stark choice: save capitalism or save the planet.

Yet isn't the choice between capitalism and our future a false choice? Aren't capitalists people? And so, when push comes to shove, won't capitalists and politicians refrain from intentionally doing irreversible damage to our prospects for survival? These questions assume that saving capitalism is the same thing as saving capitalists. Many on the left tell us that the conflict is between 'the 1%' and 'the 99%', and that the banks were bailed out in order to make the rich richer.

However, policy makers have shown no compunction about crushing businesses and individual capitalists under the wheels of the juggernaut in order to save the capitalist system. When the Federal Reserve 'bailed out' Bear Stearns, Wall Street's fifth-largest firm, it kept the *firm* from going bankrupt by forcing its owners' shares of stock to be sold off for a small fraction of their market value. And when the US government 'bailed out' the giant mortgage-loan guarantors Fannie Mae and Freddie Mac, their *owners* received none of the money, and their shares of stock have lost more than 99% of their value since the crisis erupted. In these and other cases, the government has been acting to prevent the failure of 'systemically important institutions' and to restore confidence in the system. If the institutions' owners have to be sacrificed, so be it.

The difference between the interests of capitalism and the interests of people, including the capitalists and the 1%, is what makes the intersection of ecological crisis and economic crisis so dangerous. It is why Ibrahim's analyses and proposals demand our attention. The total alienation of an economic system from human interests of any sort is a clear sign that it needs to perish and make way for a higher social order.

Andrew Kliman, New York City
February 2012

Andrew Kliman is Professor of Economics at Pace University in New York and author of *The Failure of Capitalist Production: Underlying Causes of the Great Recession* (2011) and *Reclaiming Marx's "Capital": A Refutation of the Myth of Inconsistency* (2007).

CHAPTER 1

Introduction

While the actions of mankind over the past thousand years
have had a detrimental effect on the environment, it wasn't
until the Industrial Revolution that such effect became
geologically significant – so much so that two eminent
scientists, Paul Crutzen and Eugene Stoermer, proposed
in a paper published in 2000 that this age be called the
'Anthropocene', 'the recent age of man', on the grounds
that human activities have brought about profound and
fundamental changes to the planet.

It is no coincidence that environmental degradation should
have reached the crisis level it is at today at the same time as
capitalism experiences one of the worst crises in its history.
As CO_2 pollution rose to its highest recorded level,[1] Lehman

---

1. In 2008, the Hawaii Mauna Loa Observatory warned that levels of CO_2
   in the atmosphere stood at 387 parts per million, up almost 40% since
   the Industrial Revolution and the highest level recorded for at least the last
   650,000 years.

Brothers filed for bankruptcy and the crisis that has been dubbed the 'Credit Crunch' took hold. But the Credit Crunch (and the subsequent economic and sovereign debt crises) is no ordinary crisis.

This book will demonstrate that, unlike past crises (which sooner or later blew away), the crisis that the global economy faces as it enters the second decade of the 21st century is not a passing phase, but a permanent feature in which governments continuously ensure capital's profitability through austerity measures, bail-outs and quantitative easing. It is like a boat that has developed a leak; it may not sink, but you forever have to bail the water out – calmly in placid seas, frantically in choppy waters.

Any capacity that capitalism may have had to save the planet is today highly compromised by its need to extricate itself from a deepening economic and financial crisis, the like of which has never been witnessed.[2] 'For the better part of 200 years, industrial firms engaged in what might be described as "take, make, waste" as an organising paradigm' wrote Stuart Hart of Cornell University.[3] This organising paradigm becomes even more entrenched at times of crisis, and if it is a choice

---

2. 'This is undoubtedly the biggest financial crisis the world has ever faced and it has continued now for four years. I do not know when it will come to an end', Mervyn King, Governor of the Bank of England speaking on Channel 4 News, 6 October 2011.

3. Stuart L Hart, *Capitalism at the Crossroads*, Wharton School Publishing, 2007, p5.

between saving capitalism and saving the planet, protection of the capitalist economy is deemed top priority. Witness how agreements limiting CO_2 emissions have been so readily forgotten and abandoned following the 2008 financial crisis.

* * *

There is now widespread scepticism about capitalism's ability to combat global warming. The Credit Crunch and the subsequent sovereign debt crisis have dented people's belief in the market. George Monbiot, one of the more prominent environmentalists and *Guardian* columnist, made no bones about his disillusionment. In 2008 he wrote: 'the government could set, by a certain date, a maximum level for carbon pollution per megawatt-hour for electricity production... Then ... it could leave the rest to the market.'[4] A year later, and anticipating the failure of the UN Climate Change Conference at Cancun, he wrote:

'All I know is that we must stop dreaming about an institutional response that will never materialise and start facing a political reality we've sought to avoid.'[5]

The consensus that the market is the vehicle through which reduction in greenhouse gas emission is achieved is in serious doubt. The market that can't secure its own creations (Barings

---

4. *Guardian*, 5 August 2008.
5. *Guardian*, 21 September 2010.

and Northern Rock among many others) can hardly be expected to save 'God's' creation – the planet itself. Far from saving the planet, the market, faced with a financial and economic meltdown, has no choice but to exploit the planet in a more intensive and comprehensive manner to save itself.

There is abundant criticism of the market. It ranges from inequality, unemployment and poverty to colonialism, imperialist wars and over-exploitation of natural resources. It comes from Marxists and socialists as well as those on the right who talk of the 'excesses' of capitalism. Yet it is not criticism that is required, but a critique.

* * *

The recently observed phenomenon of global warming is a result of an incremental quantitative increase in the concentration of greenhouse gases in the planet's atmosphere, which reduces the amount of the Sun's energy radiating back into space. The Earth's atmosphere, which contains CO_2 and other greenhouse gases, is transparent to sunlight, and sunlight passes through it largely unhindered, warming the Earth's surface. The warm surface then radiates heat back towards the atmosphere. However, the wavelength of this radiation is much longer than that of sunlight and cannot readily pass through the atmosphere. Some of this radiation is absorbed in the upper atmosphere and re-emitted, with about half of the re-emitted energy returning to the Earth's surface. The concentration of greenhouse gases in the atmosphere determines the amount of radiation returning to Earth.

'It is estimated that in the absence of carbon dioxide in the atmosphere, the temperature of the Earth's surface would be about twenty degrees Celsius less than it is today, while if the present amount of carbon dioxide was to be doubled, the Earth's temperature would rise between five and ten degrees Celsius which would endanger the delicate balance on which life depends.'[6]

The global ecosystem requires a certain presence of greenhouse gases – mainly water vapour (H_2O), carbon dioxide (CO_2), methane (CH_4), and nitrous oxide (N_2O) – to act as an insulating blanket, trapping sufficient solar energy to keep the global average temperature in a pleasant range; not too cold like Mars or too hot like Venus. It isn't greenhouse gas emission as such that's the problem (cows after all have been producing methane gas for centuries), but its quantity. As the release of these gases into the atmosphere quickens its pace, a tipping point is reached at which a qualitative change begins to take place.

In the field of the environment, there are several examples of where small but unremitting incremental quantitative changes have led to a qualitative transformation. Air pollution, for instance, was at the beginning localised to the immediate vicinity of a cotton mill or a coal mine. However, over the years the atmosphere of towns and cities has been transformed, the most striking examples being the London smog of the late

---

6. Alastair IM Rae, *Quantum Physics*, Oneworld, 2005, pp74–5.

1950s and early 1960s, and today's car pollution, causing smog over cities such as Beijing and Los Angeles.

* * *

The science behind the causes of global warming and climate change is indisputable and clear. Since the Industrial Revolution – a miniscule period of time in ecological terms – energy that has been stored in fossil fuels over hundreds of millions of years has been released. Since energy cannot be dissipated (just transformed) it has to go somewhere, so it goes into the atmosphere, creating the conditions for global warming.[7] The warnings are clear: the Earth is heating up on an accelerating scale.[8] The Intergovernmental Panel on Climate Change (IPCC) reported in 2007 that the years between 1995 and 2006 rank among the 12 warmest years since 1850. Meanwhile, greenhouse gas emissions have been building up faster than the worst scenarios projected by the IPCC in 1995.[9]

---

7. 'There are strong indications that the burning of fossil fuels is resulting in a gradual rise in the Earth's temperature', Alastair IM Rae, *Quantum Physics*, Oneworld, 2007, pp72–3.

8. 'Greenhouse gas emissions increased by a record amount last year to the highest carbon output in history, putting hopes of holding global warming to safe levels all but out of reach, according to unpublished estimates from the International Energy Agency', *Guardian*, 30 May 2011.

9. *Climate Change 2007: Synthesis Report*, IPCC, 2007, and *IPCC Second Assessment Report: Climate Change*, 1995.

Sea levels have risen by an average of 1.8mm per year since 1961 as a result of melting glaciers and ice caps.[10] In 2009, the Royal Society stated:

'The accumulation of carbon dioxide in the atmosphere will lead to long-term changes in the climate system that will persist for millennia. Our growing understanding of the balance of carbon between the atmosphere, oceans and terrestrial systems tells us that the greater the accumulation of carbon dioxide in the atmosphere, the greater the risk of long-term damage to Earth's life support systems. Known or probable damage includes ocean acidification, loss of rain forests, degradation of ecosystems, and desertification. These effects will lead to loss of biodiversity and reduced agricultural productivity. Reducing emissions of greenhouse gases can substantially limit the extent and severity of long-term climate change.'[11]

In contrast to the startling clarity of the warning, the response has been woefully inadequate. The solutions range from 'green taxes' and 'carbon trading' to foreign aid and the abandonment of GDP as the measure of the health of the economy. All fall within the confines and restraints of the capitalist mode of production – a system that is incessantly expansive and inherently wasteful; the precise opposite of what is required to

10. Recent climate observations compared to projections, *Science*, May 2007.
11. Royal Society, *UK Climate Science* statement, 26 November 2009.

combat climate change. This book will argue that attempting to mitigate environmental degradation, rising sea levels and global warming is irreconcilable with meeting the needs (or wants) of the market.

* * *

Capitalism has in the past been called upon to constrain its activities and reform its behaviour for the greater good. In England in the early and mid-19th century, untreated sewage from a rapidly growing urban population and sprawling industrial development polluted major rivers in towns and cities, resulting in widespread diseases and serious threats of epidemics. The government had to intervene and the worst effects of capital's bare instincts were constrained and regulated. Three Public Health Acts were passed: 1848, 1872 and 1875 – introducing basic public sanitation, and the appointment of a local medical officer, and making local authorities responsible for lighting, water supply, sewage disposal, parks, toilets and housing. The 1875 Artisans and Labourers Dwellings Act gave local authorities the power to demolish areas of housing with inadequate drainage or sewage disposal facilities. Low wages and appalling working conditions (especially for women and children) brought about the Factory Acts, which regulated the working week, and the Trade Union Acts, which provided for trade union representation.

The fact that these reforms had to be fiercely fought for is not the point. They were achieved, and capitalism's excesses were contained – its carnivorous appetite for profit dulled. The nationalisations of public utilities and of what are commonly referred to as the 'commanding heights'[12] of the economy (coal mines in 1938, electricity generation in 1947, and railways in 1948, among many others) were further examples of the possibility of reining in primitive capitalist instincts. Foreign investment was regulated with various mechanisms including foreign exchange controls.

However, in the recent past all these reforms have been rolled back, one by one. In Britain, public utilities have been privatised, exchange controls removed and trade union rights repealed. Today, Britain has the most punitive and restrictive trade union laws of any developed country and capital stands almost as deregulated as it was in the 19th century. Gone are the nationalised industries. What Harold Macmillan, a previous Tory Prime Minister, called the 'family silver'[13] was sold to any bidder regardless of national base.[14]

---

12. The origin of the phrase 'commanding heights' is attributed to a speech by Vladimir Lenin in 1922, referring to the control of key segments of a national economy. It was appropriated by the British Fabians and later adopted around the world by developing nations.

13. Harold Macmillan speaking at a dinner of the Tory Reform Group, 8 November 1985.

14. 'In Britain, in the 1980s, a total of £60 billion of state assets were sold at knock-down prices to the private sector', Ankie Hoogvelt, *Globalization and the Postcolonial World*, Palgrave, 2001, p152.

A similar process took place in Europe[15] and elsewhere.[16] For developing economies, privatisation was enforced by the International Monetary Fund (IMF) and the World Bank.[17] Today we see the IMF openly marching into countries such as Ireland and Greece demanding that they privatise state assets if they are to be bailed out of their sovereign debt.

While it is true that capitalism has been able to accommodate various reforms in the past, it certainly seems to be unable to do so now, otherwise why have they been abandoned, from the late 1970s onward? And why have they not been restored by succeeding governments? Why, in short, has Keynesian economics been replaced by neo-liberalism? Was it purely a question of personalities, changing government policies, or something more fundamental than that? If it was the former, then why have the Labour governments of

---

15. 'Fifteen years ago, the French State held majority control stakes in 37 of the top 50 enterprises in France; it now (2000) controls 12 and the number will fall further', Adair Turner, *Just Capital*, Pan, 2000, p192.

16. 'By 1992, more than 80 countries around the world had privatised some 6800 previously state-owned enterprises, mainly monopoly suppliers of essential public services such as water, electricity and telecommunications... In total, the value of global privatisation in the developing and former socialist world amounted to over US$58 billion between 1988 and 1995', Ankie Hoogvelt, *Globalization and the Postcolonial World*, Palgrave, 2001, p153.

17. 'Officials with the World Bank and the IMF had always made policy recommendations when they handed out loans.' These recommendations were based on 'such bald ideological claims as all "state enterprises should be privatised" and "barriers impeding the entry of foreign firms should be abolished"', Naomi Klein, *The Shock Doctrine*, Penguin Books, 2007, p163.

Blair and Brown continued with the same policies as their predecessor Conservative governments? In fact, Thatcher's policies can be traced back to the government of her Labour predecessor, James Callaghan. It is clear that the economic policies of various governments form a continuum, regardless of which party happens to be in power.

This book will argue that it is an illusion to think that capitalism can be prevailed upon, cajoled, reformed or regulated to take the necessary steps to control global warming; that capitalism has entered a critical zone, perched at the 'edge of a vortex',[18] where the availability of capital falls far short of that which is needed to maintain profits. Capitalism at such a precarious juncture is preoccupied with saving itself; the last thing on its mind would be saving the planet.

* * *

Nevertheless, and in spite of overwhelming evidence to the contrary, prominent environmental writers and activists, not to mention economists and politicians, continue to maintain a strong faith in the market, some with caution, and others with enthusiasm.[19] Raghuram Rajan in his award-winning

---

18. Fawzi Ibrahim, Edge of a Vortex, *Communist Review*, Autumn 2008.
19. 'Eco-effectiveness sees commerce as the engine of change and honours its need to function quickly and productively', William McDonough and Michael Braungart, *Cradle to Cradle*, North Point Press, 2002, p150. 'I do not accept that irreconcilable incompatibility [between corporations and sustainable development]', Jonathon Porritt, *Capitalism as if the World Matters*, Earthscan, 2007, p280.

book *Fault Lines*, a book dedicated to analysing the causes of what the Institute for Fiscal Studies called the 'Great Recession', begins with a statement of faith: 'I believe that the basic ideas of the free-enterprise system are sound.'[20] With this simple statement, that which is to be put in the spotlight is conveniently dispensed with as a suitable subject for investigation. It is like someone investigating the fault lines in Christianity asserting his belief that the basic ideas of the virgin birth and resurrection are sound.

New models are offered to persuade corporations that it is in 'their interest' to go green, including 'business for social responsibility', 'natural capitalism', 'sustainable global enterprise' and 'green profitability'. And of course there are countless proposals to skew the 'market' to go green, such as green taxes,[21] 'polluter pays', carbon trading and carbon credits.

Most, if not all, of these measures are biased against the poor. Take carbon credits for instance. Each year everyone would get equal carbon credits to spend, with those exceeding their quotas able to buy credits from people who use less credit. It sounds egalitarian (after all, everyone gets an equal amount of carbon credit). But like all equality of the unequal, it is a sham. It is nothing more than a licence for the rich to pollute at will at the expense of the poor, who have to suffer

---

20. Raghuram G Rajan, *Fault Lines*, Princeton, 2010, p4.

21. 'Disposable razors and nappies could be taxed as luxury goods in order to cut the amount of waste going into landfill', reported the *Independent on Sunday*, 1 August 2008.

the effects of not just their own reduced carbon footprint but also that of the rich. In this respect it is not different from the much-admired congestion charge in London and other 'green taxes'.

The *Stern Review on the Economics of Climate Change* goes as far as acknowledging a failure of the market; a failure that the report wishes to rectify:[22]

> '*Climate change is an example of market failure involving externalities and public goods. Given the magnitude and nature of the effects... it has profound implications for economic growth and development. All in all, it must be regarded as market failure on the greatest scale the world has seen.*'[23]

The solution to the 'failure of the market' is then framed in the very language of the market, namely the setting up of another market: a carbon-trading market.

Those who fail to identify the market itself as the culprit leave but one other thing to blame – the general public. Human society itself is thus blamed for its greed, wasteful

---

22. The review was commissioned by the Chancellor of the Exchequer, Gordon Brown, in July 2005 and was published in October 2006 to assess the economics of moving to a low-carbon global economy, and the potential of different approaches for adaptation to changes in the climate.
23. *Stern Review on the Economics of Climate Change*, 2006, Section 2.2, p25.

nature, selfishness,[24] irrationality and over-population.[25] The question must be posed: What part does a cotton mill worker, a miner or a sweatshop operative play in polluting the air in Manchester, Michigan or Mumbai? In what way are they greedy, wasteful, selfish or irrational? They are merely trying to feed themselves and their families. They are merely trying to survive in a capitalist world.

Lifestyle, simple pleasures and everyday activity are deemed culpable, as evidenced by proposals for fuel tax, carbon tax, road charges and draconian recycling dictats with equally draconian fines;[26] not to mention the moral pressure put on individuals to save energy. This sort of contempt neatly complements that of capitalism, which sees people as merely objects for exploitation.

In reality, the reduction in greenhouse gases as a result of individual action pales into insignificance when compared with the pollution caused by large corporations. To add insult

---

24. 'Ruin is the destination towards which all men rush, each pursuing his own best interest', The Tragedy of the Commons, *Science*, 13 December 1968, as quoted by Oliver Tickell, *Kyoto2*, Zed Books, 2008, p69.

25. 'Chief among the underlying causes of our planet's unease is the overgrowth of the human population and its impact on both ecosystems and human communities', Paul Ehrlich and Anne Erlich, *The Population Explosion*, Arrow Books, 1988, p11.

26. 'Householders face fines of up to £2,500 for putting the "wrong rubbish" in their bins. More than 10 councils have introduced penalties for those who put recyclable matter into general waste, or "contaminate" recycling boxes with other rubbish,' *Observer*, 12 March 2006.

to injury, these very same corporations continue to pollute the atmosphere, turn our forests into dust bowls and destroy marine life. They then demand subsidies and tax breaks from the government (that's us) for every step they are forced to take to clean up their act. And governments all over the world oblige. Demands on corporations are conditioned by the God-given right for corporations to make a profit.[27]

NEW ECONOMICS

The theoretical underpinning of market-led proposals for reducing greenhouse gas emissions and containing global warming is a new economic doctrine referred to as either 'natural capitalism' or 'natural economy'. Proponents of new economics share one thing: a blind faith in the market. Listen to Stuart Hart of the Johnson Graduate School of Management at Cornell University. In his book *Capitalism at the Crossroads* (with a Foreword by Al Gore) he makes the sweeping statement: 'Throughout human history, however,

---

27. In 2008, the planning conditions for new coal-fired power stations to be built at Kingsnorth for the German firm E.ON 'made no reference to carbon capture and storage (CCS)'. The process of setting the conditions involved emailing the draft to E.ON, with E.ON responding that the government 'has no right to withhold approval for a conventional plant. Six minutes later [the civil servant] answered thus: "Thanks. I won't include. Hope to get the set of draft conditions out today or tomorrow"', George Monbiot, *Guardian*, August 2008, p5.

wherever there have been people, there have been markets.'[28] So, according to Hart, cavemen and cavewomen had a daily market where they congregated to sell their wares, and hunter–gatherers got together in the African plains to exchange deer skins and plants; not to mention the primitive societies who did a roaring trade in the markets of African jungles.

But these primitive markets, and even their successors in early urban civilisations, were of a fundamentally different nature to the 'market' of today. The capitalist 'market' is not a glorified local market where local villagers bring their fruit and veg and other produce; it is nothing like the bazaars of the Middle East, or the merchants' markets of the Middle Ages, or even today's shopping malls. The 'market' is a market for stocks, shares and bonds. It distributes and allocates the social wealth to this or that enterprise.

This approach to political economy was finally crowned by Fukuyama's notion of 'the end of history'. Fukuyama's acclaimed thesis heralded not so much the end of history as the end of political economy and the end of analysis. The purpose was to enshrine, once and for all, the 'market' as an eternal feature of human existence, part and parcel of the human condition. The market (a euphemism for capitalism) has become an article of faith and, like any other faith, it is blind and cannot be questioned. That's why we have those who advocate 'natural capitalism' in agreement with advocates

28. Stuart L Hart, *Capitalism at the Crossroads*, Wharton School Publishing, 2007, p42.

of the steady-state economy, as well as those who advocate sustainability, eco-effectiveness, carbon trading and green taxation.[29]

Jonathon Porritt, a very well-regarded environmentalist, dispenses with capitalism altogether. He redefines capital as 'a stock of anything that has the capacity to generate a flow of benefits which are valued by humans',[30] which leads to his 'five capital framework', among which is natural capital: 'Historically, the first type of capital was undoubtedly natural capital.' So, according to this thesis, there was capital even in the Stone Age when man lived in caves. If only the cavemen knew it, they would have become capitalists! With his second capital, 'human capital', even labour turns into capital. But a definition of capital, if it is to be of any value, must show how it relates to capitalism, the system of production and exchange that it gave its name to. To define capital in any other way would be like defining a star as a 'prominent performer' when discussing cosmology. This is why Adam Smith defines capital as the part of the capitalist's stock that 'afford(s) him ... revenue'.[31] By revenue he, of course, means profit.

---

29. 'Future economic progress can best take place in democratic, market-based systems of production and distribution', Paul Hawken, Amory Lovins and L Hunter Lovins, *Natural Capitalism*, Back Bay Books, 1999, p9.

30. Jonathon Porritt, *Capitalism as if the World Matters*, Earthscan, 2007, p138.

31. 'His whole stock, therefore, is distinguished into two parts. That part which, he expects, is to afford him this revenue, is called his capital. The other is that which supplies his immediate consumption', Adam Smith, *Wealth of Nations*, Book II, Ch I, para 2.

The 'market'

Under capitalism 'the market' allocates the resources. Owners of capital, be they individuals, corporations or institutions, decide which investments they support and which they spurn. They are committed and sometimes required by law to obtain maximum return on their investment. In the process of resource allocation, the ordinary person in the street has no say, in spite of the fact that the wealth that is being dished out to this or that enterprise is social wealth, created by society.

Just observe how some utility corporations justify lower taxes and/or higher prices by the need to invest. In a letter to the *Guardian*, David Porter, Chief Executive of the Association of Electricity Producers objected to a windfall tax because 'it would take money out of the electricity industry just as it is planning to raise huge sums for investment in vital new infrastructure'.[32] But the money the electricity industry wishes to invest is not their money, but our money, the consumers' money. The same argument is put forward when utility corporations such as water and gas wish to raise prices above the rate of inflation.

The government, which is supposed to represent society and upon which so much hope is placed, uses society's money gathered in taxes to ensure high profits for capitalists in the form of subsidies, tax breaks and, in the case of the Private Finance Initiative, unadulterated handover of social wealth

---

32. Letters page, *Guardian*, 8 August 2008.

to the corporate sector. Governments see as their duty the protection of corporations' profits abroad through intelligence gathering, subversion and war.[33] To all of this add the enormous 2008–09 and subsequent multi-billion pound bail-out of the financial sector.

The operation of the 'market' depends on a fast return of the wages paid to workers back to the capitalist; the faster the better. Marx and Engels put it this way:

'No sooner is the exploitation of labour by the manufacturer, so far, at an end, that he receives his wages in cash, than he is set upon by the other portions of the bourgeoisie, the landlord, the shopkeeper, the pawnbroker, etc.'[34]

This process is exacerbated by the availability of credit by which future earnings are pledged to capitalist corporations. The tallyman of the 1930s and 40s was succeeded by the local bank manager and later by the credit card company. House ownership, which was swollen by the sale of council houses, vastly increased the level of personal credit as houses, though mortgaged to the hilt, were used as collateral. We now see the

---

33. In Iraq, US corporations were handed profitable contracts without any tendering process, including 'Halliburton and a subsidiary, KBR, which were major benefactors of the Bush administration's policy of awarding reconstruction contracts without a process of competitive tender', Suzanne Goldenberg, *Guardian*, 27 October 2003.

34. Marx and Engels, *Manifesto of the Communist Party*.

end result of this process: a phenomenon called the 'Credit Crunch'.

* * *

The debate rages on the best way to reduce greenhouse gas emissions: some are proven science-based solutions (such as renewable energy, efficiency improvements, waste reduction and eco-effective design); other proposals essentially punish the poor (such as green taxation), reward corporations (such as incentives in the form of subsidies and tax breaks) or in the case of nuclear power pose unpredictable catastrophic dangers for thousands of years.[35] One of the more pernicious 'solutions', a quintessentially capitalistic one, is what the US and the EU refer to as a clean energy source, commonly known as biofuels. They are certainly not clean,[36] and furthermore they take away land from local food production.[37]

---

35. 'A couple of years ago the US Congress established an expert commission to develop a language of symbolism capable of warning against the threats posed by American nuclear waste dumps 10,000 years from now', Professor Ulrich Beck, *Guardian*, 17 July 2008.
36. 'It would obviously be insane if we had a policy to try and reduce greenhouse gas emissions through the use of biofuels that's actually leading to an increase in the greenhouse gases from biofuels', Professor Robert Watson, the government's environment scientist, speaking on Radio 4's *Today* programme, 24 March 2008.
37. 'Kenneth Richter, biofuels campaigner at Friends of the Earth, said: "Biofuels ... production is wrecking rainforests, pushing up food prices and causing yet more climate-changing emissions"', *Guardian*, 5 October 2011.

Environmentalists debate fiercely in favour of this or that proposal, forgetting that none, even those grounded in science and technology, are viable if the system that's destined to deliver them is itself unviable. This book will argue that so long as these 'solutions' are based on the 'market', they are at best short term and at worst counter-productive.

The 'market' allocates resources to this or that enterprise and continually reassesses the validity of its allocation by the trading in stocks, shares and bonds. The basis of the allocation and reassessment is current and discounted prices of commodities and services. Using prices as the criteria for the allocation of resources is flawed in that it does not take into account their usefulness. The 'market' makes no distinction between medical research and research on cosmetics, between Shakespeare and pornography; if the price is right, anything goes.

How then can the 'market' favour ecologically friendly processes as opposed to short-term profiteering and 'slash and burn' economics, the time-honoured practice of capitalism. Answers come thick and fast from all quarters: reform, regulation, target setting, carbon trading and general subsidies. The idea of constraining capitalism's 'excesses' is not new. Keynes made his reputation on reforming capitalism. The lack of social responsibility of capitalism was highlighted by Conservative Prime Minister Edward Heath, who in 1973, referring to a bribery and corruption scandal involving 'Tiny' Rowland, Chief Executive of Lonrho (London and Rhodesian Mining and Land Company), coined the phrase 'the unpleasant and unacceptable face of capitalism'.[38] This of course implies that there is a pleasant and acceptable face of capitalism, which in 1973 may have been true. Heath's 'unpleasant and unacceptable face of capitalism' is today ubiquitous. In terms of social responsibility, capitalism is moving backwards, not forwards.

The question remains, can the 'market' be tamed into eco-friendly directions? I will argue later in this book that, while such constraints have been possible in the past, they are no longer a practical proposition, and in that context mainstream environmentalist movements, wittingly or unwittingly, play the role of apologist for capitalism. Their aims are laudable, the analysis lamentable. They generally blame society, humanity, wasteful habits, the 'inherently irrational and anti-ecological society'[39] or growth. Some blame governments, corporations and capitalists;[40] everyone and everything is blamed for greenhouse gas emissions, global warming and climate change, with the exception of capitalism. Here is an example:

---

38. 'It is the unpleasant and unacceptable face of capitalism, but one should not suggest that the whole of British industry consists of practices of this kind', British Prime Minister Edward Heath, speech to the British Parliament, 15 May 1973.

39. Murray Bookchin, *Towards an Ecological Society*, Black Rose Books, 1995, p92.

40. '[We] believe that governments, companies, organisations and individuals should be held accountable for abuses or complicity in abuses involving natural resources', *Global Witness*.

'That type of conclusion is likely to apply to many other collapses of past societies and to our own destiny today. We can get used to a lot of waste when the economy is good. We forget that conditions fluctuate, and we may not be able to anticipate when conditions will change. By that time we may already have become attached to an expensive lifestyle, leaving an enforced diminished lifestyle or bankruptcy as the sole "outs".'[41]

* * *

Parallels are often drawn between, on one hand, the collapse of ancient civilisations (Mesopotamia, Rome and Greece) and more recent societies (Maya and Polynesian) and on the other hand the prospects for our own civilisation today. As far as environmental collapse is concerned, the Easter Island society is often used as an example of a society that 'destroyed itself by over-exploiting its own resources'.[42] Jared Diamond, among others, draws parallels between Easter Island and today's world:

'Polynesian Easter Island was as isolated in the Pacific Ocean as the Earth is today in space... People see the collapse of Easter Island society as a metaphor, a worst-case scenario, for what may lie ahead of us in our own future.'[43]

---

41. Jared Diamond, *Collapse*, Penguin Books, 2006, p156.
42. Ibid, p118.
43. Ibid, p119.

However, civilisations and societies have collapsed for
a number of reasons, including depletion of resources,
insurmountable catastrophes, and conflict, including civil war,
as well as over-exploitation of natural resources.

Past civilisations did not exist in a vacuum. They were
characterised by their economic systems which themselves were
determined by their knowledge of agriculture, tools, etc. It is
highly unwise (not to say unscientific) not to recognise the
differences in the socioeconomic relations that defined such
civilisations.

Take the Polynesians, for instance, and the inhabitants of
Easter Island in particular. They had no metals and depended
on stone and wood for their tools. The economy was based on
the cultivation of a number of tubers and fruits, together with
an intensive exploitation of marine resources:

*'Cereals were not cultivated in Polynesia, and rice and millet
... were absent. Furthermore, the only domesticated animals
were the pig, dog and chicken, and these were rarely major
sources of meat... The most widespread system of cultivation
in Polynesia was shifting horticulture... A plot would be
planted for two or three years and then left to revert to fallow
... for perhaps ten or fifteen years. Plots were not tilled and
the Polynesians did not use the plough.'*[44]

---

44. Peter Bellwood, *The Polynesians*, Thames and Hudson, 1987, pp34–7.

There was no external trade and, with the absence of metal, timber was extensively used in construction and canoe building, as well as for tools, rope, etc. It was an economy based on scarce and limited resources, hence the compulsion for intensive deforestation and over-exploitation of marine resources just to survive.

Contrast the scarcity of Easter Island with the abundance of today. Enough food is produced in the world today to adequately feed all of its population.[45] The over-exploitation of natural resources was necessary to save the Easter Islanders from immediate starvation, in the same way as a starving farmer and his family would eat the seeds meant for next season's plantation. Today's over-exploitation is not to save humanity from starvation, but to save capitalism from liquidation.

Attention must be paid to the distinctive economic relationships of one society compared with another – the hunter–gatherer versus the subsistence farmer, ancient Greeks versus the Elizabethans, or global capitalism versus Polynesian society – and, by this means, an investigation can be made of the contemporary mode of production to determine whether it has the capacity or inclination to put a halt to climate change.

---

45. According to the UN Food and Agriculture Organisation (FAO), world agriculture produces 17% more calories per person today than it did 30 years ago, despite a 70% population increase. This is enough to provide everyone in the world with at least 2720 kilocalories (kcal) per person per day (FAO, 2002, p9).

This book will argue that capitalism is not capable of this, not because of failure of institutions, ineffective policies, absence of leadership or even lack of good intentions, but because of current capitalism's inherent contradiction.

In the 1980s Keynesianism lost out to neo-liberalism because the former outlived its usefulness just as neo-liberalism lost out to interventionism in the aftermath of the 2008 financial crash. The neo-liberals' attempt to breathe life into capitalism has been as successful as attempting to restore youthful looks to an ageing actor; brilliant in its immediate effect, but Dorian-Gray-type cracks will ultimately win out.

The much-neglected and maligned theory of the tendency of the rate of profit to fall (mainly associated with Marx) has its roots with Adam Smith[46] and David Ricardo,[47] and it is now beginning to come into its own. This book will show that if the rate of profit has a tendency to fall, then, coupled with increasingly high levels of capital accumulation, a threshold is reached, which, if crossed, makes production for profit unviable. At this stage, capital enters a 'critical zone', poised at the edge of a vortex – one wrong move and it is the end. This is 21st-century capitalism.

---

46. 'Adam Smith had treated the falling rate of profit at some length some seventy five years before Marx', Joseph M Gillman, *The Falling Rate of Profit*, Cameron Associates, 1958, p2.

47. 'We should also expect that, however, the rate of the profits of stock might diminish in consequence of the accumulation of capital on the land, and the rise of wages', David Ricardo, *On the Principles of Political Economy and Taxation*, Ch 6, para 34.

Urgent steps then have to be taken to rescue capital and restore profitability. At the critical zone, profit, which, bourgeois economists argue, is a reward for risk taking, can only be sustained through expensive and extensive government rescues, subsidies and bail-outs. Hopes of constraining and reforming capitalism are dashed as the reforms of the past are reversed.

This book will show that in the UK, the economy crossed the critical zone threshold in the 1973–74 crisis. From that point onwards, measures taken by successive governments were just one giant rescue plan: Healey's IMF loan and the subsequent public expenditure cuts (1973–79), Thatcher's privatisation (worth £60 billion),[48] financial deregulation, trade union legislation, wage cuts and de-industrialisation[49] (1979–97), and Blair/Brown's Public–Private Partnership (worth £51 billion), further deregulation and privatisation, further de-industrialisation,[50] and most recently the infamous bail-outs (2008–11).

The current high level of sovereign debt is used as the justification for severe austerity measures. That the country is in debt is undeniable. Contrary to accepted wisdom, however,

---

48. 'In Britain, in the 1980s, a total of £60bn of state assets were sold at knock-down prices to the private sector', Ankie Hoogvelt, *Globalization and the Postcolonial World*, Palgrave, 2001, p152.

49. Over 2.5 million manufacturing jobs were lost between 1979 and 1997 (Office for National Statistics).

50. 'From 1978–2008, almost 4m UK manufacturing jobs were lost', *The Future of UK Manufacturing*, PricewaterhouseCoopers, 2009, Section 9.

such debts do not have to be paid back. Consider the fact that the very same people and institutions that we so heavily bailed out are the ones we are indebted to. Defaulting on sovereign debt is treated as a sin comparable only to infanticide and must not be mentioned in polite society.[51] In reality, defaulting has a glorious history; it was one of the first acts of the French Revolution. Argentina, which defaulted on £94 billion in 2001 didn't spontaneously combust. Any pain and suffering that may be encountered as a consequence of defaulting pale into insignificance when compared with the austerity measures that people are forced to endure;[52] a one-off in the case of defaulting and a recurring, if not a permanent, theme to avoid a default.

STRUCTURE OF THE BOOK

Following the Introduction, Chapter 2 'From the Industrial Revolution to Environmental Pollution' traces the present

---

51. Non-payment of sovereign debt is enshrined in legal theory; it is known as 'odious debt': 'This is a legal theory, established in the 1920s, which holds that national debt incurred by a government for purposes that do not serve the best interests of the nation should not be enforceable', Jason Manolopoulos, *Greece's Odious Debt*, Anthem Press, 2011, pxiv.
52. In 2011, in order to avoid a default, the Greek government agreed an eye-watering austerity package which involved cutting €14.32bn of public spending, putting 30,000 civil servants on 12 months' notice with a 60% pay cut, cutting pensions by between 20% and 40% and raising €310m through reduced spending on health, and €50bn from privatisations, as well as raising €14.09bn in taxes over five years.

environmental degradation back to the Industrial Revolution, the birth of modern-day capitalism. The damage done to the environment over the past 200 years has been so significant that, in a move that has no precedent, eminent geologists have proposed a new epoch to mark that period – the 'Anthropocene'. This chapter asks if our planet's environmental woes are a result of human activity in general or whether it is the existing economic system that lies behind global warming and climate change. The chapter argues that population growth as such is not a cause of greenhouse gas emissions and climate change, since the more populated regions of the world emit the lowest levels of greenhouse gases. It points out that a high level of greenhouse gas emission bears a robust correlation to commodity production.

The following two chapters examine the different solutions to combating environmental degradation on offer, from the UN to the so-called Green Lobby, pressure groups and environmentalists, and asks: can capitalism be tamed?

This part of the book starts with '*The Illusions of New Economics*', Chapter 3, which investigates the theoretical underpinnings of these proposals and questions their validity. It takes issue with 'natural capitalism', the idea that 'natural resources and living systems' must be assigned a value,[53] and argues that by giving a value to free natural resources, nature is turned into a commodity ripe for exploitation and profit making. The chapter goes on to question the validity and

---

53. Paul Hawken, et al, *Natural Capitalism*, Back Bay Books, 1999, p5.

consistency of the concepts used by the proponents of new economics (such as Hawken, Lovins, Porritt and others) and argues that their underlying message is that capitalism is the natural order of things. The chapter uses flow diagrams to represent the economic system and shows that including 'considerations of natural environment' in the capitalist process does not constrain capitalist exploitation, but increases profits.

The fundamental principles behind the capitalist system of production and exchange is summarised in Chapter 4, 'Re-claiming the Classicists: Adam Smith, David Ricardo and Karl Marx'. It takes issue with those, such as recent 'ecological economists', who arbitrarily impose their own rules on the economy and expect the system to obey them. The chapter traces the origin of the labour law of value to Adam Smith, David Ricardo and Karl Marx and explains its central role in a capitalist economy. The chapter then demonstrates that the theory that the rate of profit tends to fall (though dismissed and maligned by many) is not only sound theoretically, but is also backed up by empirical evidence.

It goes on to explain how the toxic combination of vast capital accumulation and pressure on the rate of profit to fall inevitably leads to the economy entering a 'critical zone' in which production for profit becomes unviable and the system has to be urgently and decisively rescued.

Chapter 5, 'Saviours of the Environment or Apologists for Capitalism?', takes issue with those who argue that capitalism is irrational and wish to reform it with regulation and taxation. It maintains that capitalism is as rational as photosynthesis, in that both processes operate according to internal laws that govern conduct that cannot be wished away. The chapter challenges such concepts as the 'tyranny of the bottom line', 'the fetishism of growth' and the 'post-growth economy'.

Chapter 6, 'A Crisis Too Far', maintains that the current crisis of capitalism is not the 1930s all over again – it is far worse. It argues that the belief that one can make capitalism constrain its behaviour at a time of crisis is illusory. It contends that the Credit Crunch is not a passing phase but a permanent feature and asks: is there a future under capitalism?

If capitalism cannot be tamed and regulated to do the right thing, are we doomed? Chapter 7, 'Post-capitalist Economy', argues that, far from being the natural order of things, capitalism, like all other economic systems that preceded it, is but a passing phase that is waiting to be superseded. It argues that the embryo of a new post-capitalist society is present in the womb of the old economy and contends that 'proletarian professionalism', the pride, dignity and self respect which accompanies a skilled workforce, haunts the capitalist order.

Using the labour law of value, it argues that a post-capitalist society is a non-commodity economy where the law of value no longer operates. It looks at the 'cash-free' internal economy of the pre-reform NHS as an example of a non-commodity economy and shows how labour time, and not labour value, is used to organise its work pattern. It concludes that, under a non-commodity economy, looking after the environment will change from an ancillary to an integral part of the production process.

Finally, Chapter 8, '*Capitalism versus Planet Earth – An Irreconcilable Conflict*', argues that in the post-2007 financial/economic crisis, and with capital in the 'critical zone', governments see their first priority as saving the economy, leaving the environment a very distant second. This was demonstrated by the failure of the 2011 Durban Conference to establish binding commitments to reduce greenhouse gases in the atmosphere. It concludes that it is not possible to reconcile the insatiable desires of capital to expand and reduce costs with the need for renewable energy and sustainable living.

CHAPTER 2

From the Industrial Revolution to Global Pollution

In May 2000, Paul Crutzen and Eugene Stoermer wrote a short paper suggesting that the Holocene epoch had ended and a new geological epoch which they named the 'Anthropocene' had begun:[1]

> *'This is the period when data retrieved from glacial ice cores show the beginning of a growth in the atmospheric concentrations of several "greenhouse" gases'.*

They assigned the latter part of the 18th century (the start of the Industrial Revolution in England, coinciding with James Watt's invention of the steam engine in 1784) as the onset of the Anthropocene. In this way, the new epoch has been

---

1. Paul Crutzen and Eugene Stoermer, *IGBP Newsletter* 41, May 2000.

irrevocably linked to the capitalist system of production and exchange – the market economy.

It's not uncommon in such discourse that Crutzen and Stoermer's insight should attract supporters as well as detractors. What is unusual, however, is that both supporters and detractors should agree on who is to blame for the parlous state of our planet. Human activity in general and population growth in particular are singled out as the culprit. Statements such as 'the Anthropocene is the result of the vast expansion of human population' are common. When discussing proposals that will avoid environmental disaster, population growth and human behaviour come top of the list:

> *'[T]here are many realistic, often-discussed policies by which we could avoid disaster, such as limiting human population growth, preserving natural habitat and adopting other environmental safeguards.'* [2]

OUR EVOLUTIONARY AND SOCIOECONOMIC INHERITANCE: HOW DID WE GET TO WHERE WE ARE TODAY?

The proposal by Crutzen and Stoermer is that the planet has entered a new geological epoch comparable with such epochs as the Pleistocene (1.8–0.011 million years BP) which ended 11,000 years BP with the extinction of the mammoths and

---

2. Jared Diamond, *The Third Chimpanzee*, Harper, 2006, p366.

various other large mammals. This was a very bold proposal, with its reverberations going far beyond the International Union of Geological Sciences (IUGS), which has the actual task of approving such categorisation.[3] This is because, unlike previous allocations of periods and epochs to the Geological Time Scale, the concept of the Anthropocene carries with it a statement that our planet is in very real peril of destruction as far as life, especially of the human variety, is concerned. To appreciate the significance of the Anthropocene thesis, let's look at the place of humans in the geological evolutionary history of our planet.

Geologists divide the geological history of the Earth into eras, periods, epochs and ages. Above eras are eons and supereons. It is estimated that the Earth was formed 4.6 billion (4,600 million) years before the present (BP), and life in the form of microscopic bacteria and algae began in the Hadean eon some 3.6 billion (3,600 million) years BP, with photosynthesis appearing 600 million, complex cells 1,600 million and multicellular life 2,000 million years later. Simple animals evolved 600 million years BP, with fish evolving 500 million, land plants 470 million, insects 400 million, amphibians 360 million, reptiles 300 million, mammals 200 million, birds 150 million, and flowers 130 million years BP.

The first vertebrate land animals inhabited the Earth some 380 million years BP, followed by the dinosaurs, which

---

3. To date (2012) the IUGS is yet to determine if the Anthropocene will be formally accepted into the Geological Time Scale.

appeared 230 million years BP. The dinosaurs became extinct at the end of the Mesozoic era and the beginning of the Cenozoic (new life) era. The Cenozoic era spans a period from 65 million years ago to the present, divided into three periods, the last of which is the Quaternary period (beginning 2.6 million years ago).[4] The beginning of the Cenozoic marks an abrupt transition from the age of the reptiles to the age of the mammals.

The Quaternary period encompasses the two latest epochs: the Pleistocene (1.8 million–11,000 years BP) and the Holocene (11,000 years BP). The Quaternary sees the emergence of the genus Homo: Homo erectus 1.8 million years ago, and Homo sapiens 500,000 years ago. 'Behavioural modernity' and the 'Great Leap Forward',[5] when speech and the ability to communicate evolved, have been dated at only 40,000 years ago.

Alongside the evolution of man and the advances made by mankind came new economic and social forms. The evolution and revolution of socioeconomic structures began when

---

4. The system for the naming of periods is constantly changing as more information is collected and analysed. Although the Quaternary period is no longer an official geological time period, having been superseded by a larger Neocene period, it is still commonly used for the most recent period in geological time.

5. Jared Diamond, 2006, op cit. Diamond, a physiologist at UCLA, labelled this evolutionary change the 'Great Leap Forward'. He postulates that the Great Leap Forward occurred approximately 40,000 years ago. Prior to that, man possessed tools and a sizeable brain, but little progress had occurred for hundreds of thousands of years.

humankind left its nomadic existence and began to settle with the development of agriculture. Early agriculture is generally traced back 10,000 years BP. Until then, most humans were hunter–gatherers living in small nomadic groups that formed what are known as band societies. The transition from hunting and gathering to arable agriculture and animal husbandry, known as the Neolithic revolution, prompted a rudimentary form of division of labour and specialisation:

> *'Agriculture and herding … made it possible to feed more people per square mile of land than could live on wild foods available in the same area. Storable food surpluses grown by some individuals permitted other individuals to devote themselves to metallurgy, manufacturing, writing – and to serving in full-time professional armies. Domestic animals provided not only meat and milk to feed people, but also wool and hides to clothe people, and power to transport people and goods. Animals also provided power to pull ploughs and carts, and thus to increase agricultural productivity greatly over that previously attainable by human muscle power alone.'*[6]

Access to surplus food as a result of agriculture, the domestication of animals and the use of metal tools led to the formation of permanent human settlements. Agriculture encouraged trade and cooperation, as well as conflicts and wars.

---

6. Jared Diamond, 2006, op cit, p237. Surprisingly, Diamond is reluctant to use the concept of division of labour.

The division of labour was at this stage still very elementary with a corresponding elementary social structure of patriarchal chieftains, tribe members and slaves. With the ancient civilisations of Mesopotamia (6,000 years BP), Egypt (5,000 years BP) and the Indus Valley (5,000 years BP), a more complex economic and social order developed, comprising nobles (rulers), labourers (including merchants) and slaves. Ancient Greece and Rome exhibited similar class structures, with upper, middle, lower and slave classes for Greece, and patrician, plebeian and slave for Rome.

The Middle Ages saw the evolution of the feudal system, with large feudal lords owning huge tracts of land with serf labour chained to it. In the towns, artisans and merchants formed themselves into guilds to protect themselves against the nobility and the influx of serfs into towns.

'The organisation of both (landed property and individuals with small capital) was determined by the restricted conditions of production – the small-scale and primitive cultivation of the land, and the craft type of industry. There was little division of labour in the heyday of feudalism.

Although we come across the first beginnings of capitalist production as early as the 14th or 15th century, sporadically, in certain towns of the Mediterranean, the capitalistic era dates from the 16th century.'[7]

---

7. Engels, *The German Ideology*.

Feudalism then gave way to the capitalist system of production, first in England (in the 16th century) and later in the rest of Europe: 'Wherever it appears, the abolition of serfdom has been long effected, and the highest development of the Middle Ages, the existence of sovereign towns, has been long on the wane.'[8] In England 'the years between 1760 and 1820 are the years of wholesale enclosure, in which, village after village, common rights are lost',[9] culminating with the mass expulsion of the peasantry and agricultural labourers as common land was confiscated and arable land transformed into sheep walks for the wool industry:

> 'What was "perfectly proper" in terms of capitalist property-relations involved, none the less, a rupture of the classical integument of village custom and of right: and the social violence of enclosure consisted precisely in the drastic, total imposition upon the village of capitalist property definitions.'[10]

In *Capital*, Marx remarked: 'The prelude of the revolution that laid the foundation of the capitalist mode of production was played in the last third of the 15th, and the first decade of the 16th century.' Referring to land enclosures, Marx wrote: 'A

---

8. Marx, *Capital*, Volume 1, Ch 26.
9. EP Thompson, *The Making of the English Working Class*, Penguin, 1970, p217.
10. Ibid, p238.

mass of free proletarians was hurled on the labour market by the breaking-up of the bands of feudal retainers.'[11]

The capitalist system of production having thus established itself moved from watermill- and windmill-powered manufacturing to machine-powered manufacture which started in the textile industries and moved to coal mining and iron making. Markets grew out of all recognition, and with the introduction of steam power in factories in the late 18th century, manufacture gave way to large-scale industrial production, ushering in what has become known as the Industrial Revolution. Trade expanded, helped by the introduction of canals and the railways.

But capitalism, unlike any other system of the past, survives only through continuous expansion as it seeks increasing investment in the pursuit of not just profits, but ever higher profits. As Milton Friedman explains: 'It is the responsibility of business to use its resources and engage in activities designed to increase its profits.'[12] The philosopher Karl Popper put it this way: 'It is true, probably, that [the capitalist] does not like to see a fall in his rate of profit. But, as long as his income does not fall, but, on the contrary, rises, there is no real danger.'[13]

The search for year-on-year increases in profit is intrinsic; witness how share prices fall when a company fails to report

---

11. Marx, *Capital*, Volume 1, Ch 27.
12. Milton Friedman, *The New York Times Magazine*, 13 September 1970.
13. Karl Popper, *The Open Society*, Vol 2, Routledge Classics, 2003, p202.

a significant increase in profit.[14] The demand for improved productivity is incessant. In the Middle Ages innovation was considered an aberration; under capitalism it became a necessity.

The period from the late 18th century saw a rapid increase in the use of energy derived from fossil fuels as the economy of the industrial world began to grow at an unprecedented rate. Today growth in the gross domestic product (GDP) of less than 2 or 3% is considered inadequate and double-figure growth is not unusual. Compare that with economies prior to the Industrial Revolution:

'For much of human history, a sustained expansion of the economy by 2% required not just a year but decades to achieve... One recent study ... estimates that in what are now the western economies, during the 1000 years between AD500 and 1500, GDP grew on average by only 0.1 per cent a year.'[15]

The per capita annual energy consumption grew by similar margins. While in ancient Greek and Roman times average annual per capita energy consumption was 0.5 tons of oil equivalent (TOE), it rose to 0.55 TOE in England in 1800,

---

14. 'Simon Wolfson, chief executive of Next, said that full-year profits would be slightly higher than expected at £502m... Next shares closed down 114p at £15.52p', *The Telegraph*, 4 January 2008.
15. Paul Ormerod, *The Death of Economics*, Wiley, 1997, pp9–10.

to reach 3.5 TOE in 2000.[16] The use of fossil fuels – first coal
and then increasingly oil and gas – completed the transition to
the high-energy economy that we have today with its gigantic
multinational industrial corporations that dominate the world
economy.

* * *

In geological terms, humans are relative newcomers:

*'If the history of the human race began at midnight then
we would now be almost at the end of the first day. We
lived as hunter-gatherers for nearly the whole of the day,
from midnight through dawn, noon and sunset. Finally at
11.54 p.m. we adopted agriculture.'*[17]

Although the journey that humans have taken since they left
Africa has been a tiny period, it, nonetheless, constituted a
dynamic evolutionary period punctuated by revolutionary
advances in science and technology as well as socioeconomic
structures, all of which were occasioned by mankind's efforts to
satisfy its wants and needs. Such accelerated periods of advance
have been concentrated in the latter part of mankind's history.

---

16. Gian Paolo Beretta, *World Energy Consumption and Resources: An Outlook for
   the Rest of the Century*, Universita di Brescia.
17. Jared Diamond, *The Third Chimpanzee*, Harper, 2006, p191.

The Anthropocene – More of a Warning than an Epoch

The case for the Anthropocene is firmly based on scientific evidence that the 'Earth has endured changes sufficient to leave a global stratigraphic signature [recognised by rock formation] distinct from that of the Holocene or of previous Pleistocene interglacial phases, encompassing novel biotic, sedimentary, and geochemical change'.[18] These changes, Paul Crutzen and Eugene Stoermer maintain, are a result of 'human activities' such as the 'expansion of mankind', extinction of species, release of climatically important greenhouse gases, loss of 50% of the world's mangroves and removal of more than 25% of the primary production of the oceans:

'Considering these and many other major and still growing impacts of human activities on earth and atmosphere ... it seems to us more than appropriate to emphasize the central role of mankind in geology and ecology by proposing to use the term "Anthropocene" for the current geological epoch.'[19]

They traced the start of the Anthropocene to the latter part of the 18th century, to 'coincide with James Watt's invention of the steam engine in 1784', thus linking the new epoch firmly to the start of the Industrial Revolution and in turn to the

---

18. Jan Zalasiewicz, et al, Are We Now Living in the Anthropocene?, *GSA Today*, February 2008.
19. Paul Crutzen and Eugene Stoermer, *IGBP Newsletter 41*, May 2000.

capitalist system that begat it. Thus Crutzen and Stoermer challenged the world to face up to the transformation of the planet by human economic and social evolution.

Prior to the Industrial Revolution, exploitation of energy was mostly limited to firewood and animal, human, water and wind power. The Industrial Revolution saw the application of steam power to the production process, increasing the scale of industrial output and later revolutionising transport. It marked a major turning point in human history, paving the way to today's extensive global exploitation of the Earth's fossil fuel resources – coal, oil and gas – to power planet-wide industry, construction and mass transport.

The Industrial Revolution brought about social as well as economic upheavals. Factory owners used cheap labour, including children, to run their machines. By the age of 6, many children were already working 14 hours a day in factories in London, Manchester and other English cities in the late 18th and early 19th century.[20] In the search for cheap raw materials and new markets for mass-produced goods, continents were invaded and their inhabitants colonised. Colonies were kept docile by inhumane repression, while wars with other colonial powers over the division of the world intensified. When the colonies fought back and got independence, they were shackled with economic domination.

---

20. A detailed account of the living conditions of the working class in England at the time may be found in Engels' *Conditions of the Working Class in England*.

The Industrial Revolution paved the way for unprecedented advances in the fields of science and technology, chemistry and medicine; from electromagnetism and the invention of the electric motor, quantum mechanics and the invention of the transistor to the splitting of the atom and the onset of nuclear power, the discovery of DNA and the genome project. However, the darker legacy of the Industrial Revolution is that it opened the way for the unprecedented, wholesale exploitation of the Earth's resources to the point of extinction.[21]

The changes that followed the Industrial Revolution encompass a variety of aspects. In their paper entitled 'Are We Now Living in the Anthropocene?' Jan Zalasiewicz and 20 other academics outlined these changes. They included population and economic growth, CO_2 emission, temperature rise, soil erosion and deforestation, extinction of species and the acidification of the oceans. For a summary, see the box below.

The sensitivity of the climate to greenhouse gases, and the scale of modern changes to flora and fauna, make it likely that 'we have entered a stratigraphic interval [a period which results in changes to rock formations] without close parallel in any previous Quaternary interglacial'.[22] The predictions for future

---

21. Jan Zalasiewicz, et al, Are We Now Living in the Anthropocene?, *GSA Today*, February 2008, and IPCC, *Regional Impact of Climate Change*, United Nations, 1997.

22. Jan Zalasiewicz, et al, Are We Now Living in the Anthropocene? *GSA Today*, February 2008.

SUMMARY OF THE IMPACT OF HUMAN ACTIVITIES ON THE ENVIRONMENT SINCE THE INDUSTRIAL REVOLUTION

Population growth: From the beginning of the Industrial Revolution to the present day, global human population has climbed rapidly from under a billion to its current 7 billion, and it continues to rise.

Economic growth: The Industrial Revolution launched the world onto a path of sustained economic growth, with unprecedented levels of trade. For the period 500–1500 annual economic growth in Western economies averaged around 0.1%. Or put another way, the economic activity of the West in 1500 was between two and a half and three times greater than in 500, a period of 1000 years. Economic activity doubled over the next 200 years (1500–1700) but started to take off following the Industrial Revolution. 'To put this in perspective, the Western economies grew as much in percentage terms between 1950 and 1970 as they did between 500 and 1500.'* Today economic activity doubles every 15 years.

Carbon cycle perturbation: The atmospheric CO_2 level (379 parts per million (ppm) in 2005) is over a third higher than in pre-industrial times and at any time in the past 900,000 years. The IPCC predicts that this level will double by the end of the 21st century. The concentration of methane in the atmosphere has already roughly doubled. These changes have been considerably more rapid than those associated with glacial–interglacial transitions.

Temperature: Global temperature rise has lagged behind the increase in greenhouse gas levels, 'perhaps as a result of industrially derived sulphate aerosols'. Nevertheless, temperatures in the past century rose overall, the rate of increase accelerating in the past two decades. There is now scientific consensus that anthropogenic carbon emissions are the cause. The IPCC predicts temperature to rise by between 1.1 °C and 6.4 °C by the end of this century, 'leading to global temperatures not encountered since the Tertiary period' which occurred 65–2.5 million years ago.

Changes to physical sedimentation: Erosion and long-term wearing away of the Earth's surface of land by human activity, 'both directly, through agriculture and construction, and indirectly, by damming most major rivers, has increased dramatically and now exceeds natural sediment production by an order of magnitude'.

Biotic changes: Humans have caused the extinction of countless animal and plant species, possibly since as early as the late Pleistocene, when a large proportion of the terrestrial megafauna disappeared. Accelerated rates of extinction and species population decline on land have spread into the shallow seas, notably on coral reefs. The rate of extinction may produce a major extinction event analogous to those that took place at the Cretaceous–Tertiary boundary (65.5 million years ago) and at other points in the Earth's history.

Ocean changes: Slight rises in sea level have been noted by the IPCC to have occurred over the past century, and are ascribed to a combination of ice melt and thermal expansion of the oceans. Relative to pre-Industrial-Revolution oceans, surface ocean waters now have a pH 0.1 lower (more acidic) due to anthropogenic carbon release.

Source: Zalasiewicz, et al, 2008, op cit, and IPCC, *Regional Impact of Climate Change*, United Nations, 1997

* Paul Ormerod, *The Death of Economics*, Wiley, 1997, p10.

levels of greenhouse gas emissions, increased ocean acidity and changes to flora and fauna are even more cataclysmic. Temperatures are predicted to rise by up to 50°C or more. Such 'temperature change will cause changes in habitat beyond environmental tolerance… These effects are permanent, as future evolution will take place from surviving stocks'.[23]

As for changes in oceans' acidity, it is projected that the effects will be physical (as excess acid is neutralised by dissolution of ocean-floor carbonate sediment) as well as biological.[24] The IPCC warns that: 'Anthropogenic warming and sea level rise would continue for centuries due to the time scales associated with climate processes and feedbacks, even if greenhouse gas concentrations were to be stabilised.'[25]

In its 1997 report, the IPCC catalogues the likely impact of climate change on the ecosystem: 'large shifts of vegetation boundaries into higher latitudes and elevations can be expected. The mix of species … will change… The long-term viability of tropical ecosystems will be compromised.' As for water resources: 'Changes in climate could exacerbate periodic and chronic shortfalls of water, particularly in arid and semi-arid areas of the world.' And food: 'Changes in climate will interact with stresses that result from actions to increase agricultural production, affecting crop yields and productivity in different ways, depending on the types of agricultural

---

23. Ibid.
24. Ibid.
25. IPCC, *Regional Impact of Climate Change*, United Nations, 1997.

practices and systems in place.' Then coastal systems: 'An estimated 46 million people per year currently are at risk of flooding from storm surges. Climate change will exacerbate these problems, leading to potential impacts on ecosystems and human coastal infrastructure.' And finally human health: 'Climate change could affect human health through increases in heat-stress mortality, tropical vector-borne diseases, urban air pollution problems, and decreases in cold-related illnesses.'

The case for a new geological epoch – the Anthropocene – is thus overwhelming; the repercussions of the associated climatic, biotic and other changes are devastating, taking the planet towards irreversible climate change[26] and threatening the viability of life itself.[27] Hence the clamber to look for the motive force behind global warming and climate change, to halt its progress and, if possible, reverse it.

One of the more vociferous detractors of the Anthropocene concept is Jared Diamond who devotes much of his book *The Third Chimpanzee* to proving that there was as much destruction of the environment before the Industrial Revolution as there has been after it, stating that '[i]t's now clear that pre-industrial societies have been exterminating species, destroying habitats and undermining their own

---

26. 'Climate change is perilously approaching irreversibility', Jules Boykoff, Associate Professor of Political Science, Pacific University, Oregon, *Guardian*, 28 June 2011.
27. Upon taking over as the new head of Greenpeace in November 2009, Kumi Naidoo said that human existence is 'fundamentally under threat'.

existence for thousands of years'[28] and, as such, nothing has really changed with the advent of wide-scale industry. It is of course true that human influence on atmospheric gas concentration and the Earth's climate began before 1800 as shown by William Ruddiman in 2003.[29] However, the rate of change in, for example, greenhouse gas concentration has been qualitatively different, of a different order of magnitude since the Industrial Revolution than at any time before it. As Jan Zalasiewicz, et al, pointed out, 'Human activity then [mid-Holocene] may help characterise Holocene strata, but it did not create new, global environmental conditions that could translate into a fundamentally different stratigraphic signal', as is the case in the Anthropocene.[30]

IS HUMANKIND GUILTY?

The consensus shared by academics and environmentalists is that mankind and its activities are the cause of our current environmental degradation, activities that some go as far as to imply to be unnatural. Statements such as 'until the beginning of the Anthropocene, the [Earth] systems were all

28. Jared Diamond, *The Third Chimpanzee*, Harper, 2006, p319.

29. William Ruddiman, *Climate Change 61*, Kluwer Academic Publishers, 2003. 'Atmospheric emissions of these gasses [CO_2 and CH_4] first altered atmospheric concentration thousands of years ago.'

30. Jan Zalasiewicz, et al, Are We Now Living in the Anthropocene?, *GSA Today*, February 2008.

natural. Now humans have begun to influence the planet, changing the operation of many systems'.[31] In other words, up to the beginning of the Anthropocene, human activity did not change the 'operation' of these systems, which remained natural and became unnatural once human activities began to influence their operation. Such statements take no account of the different economic and social structures under which 'human activity' had taken place over the past few thousand years.

Furthermore, animals' activities also have an effect on the environment in a similar way to humans. Darwin used the term 'natural' in 'natural selection' in order, he wrote, 'to mark its relation to man's power of selection'.[32] There is no implication here that the power of selection as practised by man is unnatural or results in unnatural outcomes. The only difference between human activities and those of other animals, or for that matter what insurance companies call 'acts of God', is that the former are conscious actions. Neither does the fact that human activity could damage the environment (to the detriment of their own species) make it any less natural than that of parasitoids which live off and ultimately kill their host.

Men and women do not live in some form of abstraction regardless of the prevailing socioeconomic conditions; there is no such thing as mankind as such, for man the hunter–gatherer is not the same as man the wage-earner. A

---

31. Andraea Meinrat, *Key Themes in Environmental Science*.
32. Charles Darwin, *The Origin of Species*, Wordsworth, 1998, p49.

hunter–gatherer leaves his dwelling to hunt wild animals and gather wild plants, a necessary activity for his survival. There is no question of our hunter–gatherer going to work for another hunter–gatherer. A 17th-century slave in Virginia could not leave his master to work for himself, and the only way a serf was 'liberated' from the land was when he was kicked out by the landlord when it became more profitable to turn farm land into pasture.

Apart from being inaccurate, the implication that man's activities are unnatural gives substance to those who see humanity itself (rather than the socioeconomic structure under which these activities take place) as responsible for climate change and environmental degradation. This is why growth of population tops the list of causes of increased CO_2 in the atmosphere. Jared Diamond goes further than most. He advances the theory that the evolution of modern man brought about new traits, one of which is 'our propensity to kill each other and to destroy our environment'[33] and 'our propensity for xenophobic killing of other human groups',[34] which together with the other 'black traits' are responsible for man's 'self-destructive abuse of our environment', which he describes as the 'prime mover of human history'.[35]

A more common approach is to blame our indulgent and wasteful behaviour. The blaming of humanity, whether

33. Jared Diamond, *The Third Chimpanzee*, Harper, 2006, p3.
34. Ibid, p8.
35. Jared Diamond seems to treat what he calls 'black traits' like the Bible's original sin.

in the exaggerated form of 'black traits' or under the more common heading of 'lifestyle', for the degradation of the environment serves to draw attention away from looking for genuine remedies. We end up focusing on individual action from recycling, rejecting plastic bags and 'abandoning the flush toilet',[36] reducing our carbon footprint and combating 'consumerism' to the 'inner spiritual growth' and 'wisdom and compassion' of the Buddhist Sulak Sivaraska.[37]

SOCIOECONOMIC STRUCTURES – EVOLUTION OR INVENTION?

Geologically, the Earth has always been in a process of evolution that continues today. Similarly, life on Earth has continuously changed, evolved and developed; millions of species came and disappeared as new ones took root. Every species left its mark, its impression on the Earth. In the same way, human life evolved and developed into its present-day social and economic forms and structures. These forms and structures were not invented by humans (Adam Smith did not invent capitalism, he analysed it), but evolved out of necessity in the same way that dinosaurs evolved wings to become birds.

The economic and social progress of humans from hunter–gatherer through serfdom to present-day global capitalism was

---

36. Gustavo Esteva, activist and founder of the Universidad de la Tierra, Mexico, writing in the *Guardian*, 16 December 2010.
37. Sulak Sivaraska asserts that 'the west invented (private property) and we, the Asians, dutifully have followed their lead', *The Wisdom of Sustainability*, Souvenir Press, 2011, p15.

as natural as any Darwinian evolution, in that changes in the means by which humans catered for their needs and wants brought about changes in their economic relations and social structures. Thus, arable agriculture and animal husbandry brought about early settlements. This was reflected in a new social and economic order. Similarly, at the other end of the timeline, the invention of the steam engine brought about the Industrial Revolution. The changes in CO_2 concentration, loss of biodiversity, ocean acidification, deforestation and chemical pollution that have taken place up to the present, and the projected changes in the future, can only be seen as a result of human economic and social evolution and not due to abstract humankind.

POPULATION VERSUS POLLUTION

Read the literature on the causes of environmental degradation, climate change and global warming and you will find that human population is almost invariably cited among the top three. Some commentators do so directly:

'[T]hose who fail to see that population growth and climate change are two sides of the same coin are either ignorant or hiding from the truth. These two huge environmental problems are inseparable and to discuss one while ignoring the other is irrational.'[38]

---

38. James Lovelock, *Guardian*, 28 September 2009.

Paul and Anne Ehrlich, who wrote several books about population, claim that 'Global warming, acid rain, depletion of the ozone layer, vulnerability to epidemics, and exhaustion of soils and ground-water are all ... related to population size'.[39] The IPCC describes GDP per capita and population growth as together constituting 'the main drivers of the increase in global emissions during the last three decades of the 20th century'.[40] Others blame population by association: 'From the beginning of the Industrial Revolution to the present day, global human population has climbed rapidly from under a billion to its current 6.5 billion and it continues to rise. The exploitation of coal, oil and gas in particular has enabled planet-wide industrialisation, construction, and mass transport, the ensuing changes encompassing a wide variety of phenomena.'[41]

The bare facts seem to support these assertions and implications. As Crutzen and Stoermer pointed out: 'The expansion of mankind, both in numbers and per capita exploitation of Earth's resources, has been astounding... During the past three centuries human population increased tenfold to 6000 million.' They conclude that 'mankind will remain a major geological force for many millennia, possibly millions of years, to come'.[42]

---

39. Paul and Anne Ehrlich, *The Population Explosion*, Arrow, 1991, p17.
40. United Nations, IPCC Climate Change 2007, Working Group III, *Mitigation of Climate Change*.
41. Jan Zalasiewicz, et al, Are We Now Living in the Anthropocene?, *GSA Today*, February 2008.
42. Paul Crutzen and Eugene Stoermer, *IGBP Newsletter* 41, May 2000.

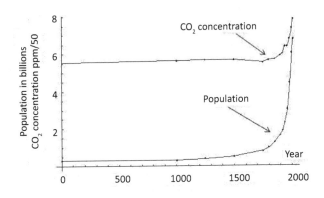

Figure 2.1 Population growth and CO_2 concentration, 500–2010

The increase in world population over the past few centuries has indeed been accompanied by a range of changes in the global environment, such as an increase in the level of atmospheric CO_2 (see Figure 2.1). However, the correlation between population and CO_2 levels cannot be assumed to be linear, as areas of high population are not necessarily areas with high CO_2 emissions as we shall see below.

In its report *The World at Six Billion* the United Nations looks at changes in human population over the past two and a half centuries. It estimates the population of the world to have been about 300 million 2000 years ago: 'For a very long time the world population did not grow significantly, with periods of growth followed by periods of decline. It took more than 1600 years for the world population to double to 600 million.' In the same report, the UN estimates the world population as 791 million in 1750. It goes on to note that 'By 1900, 150 years later, the world population had doubled, to

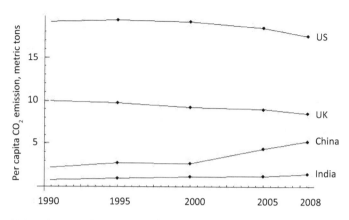

Source: United Nations Statistic Division, *The World at Six Billion*

Figure 2.2 Per capita annual CO_2 emission in metric tons

1.7 billion.'[43] Other UN data show that it then increased to 2.52 billion by 1950 and to 6.45 billion by 2005.[44] Today it stands at 7 billion.

As for changes in the planet's environment, take one measure of environmental pollution, the atmospheric concentration of CO_2. It was minuscule before the year 1000, hovered within a range of 275 to 285ppm in the pre-industrial era (1000–1750) and has climbed steadily over the last 250 years, increasing by about 100ppm (36%), to 379ppm in 2005.[45]

---

43. United Nations, *The World at Six Billion*.
44. UN data on population.
45. IPCC, 2007.

However, CO_2 emission is not uniformly distributed around the globe, with the more developed nations[46] constituting approximately 20% of the world's population responsible for nearly 60% of emissions generated to date. For the period 1850–2002, cumulative CO_2 emission, a measure which weighs all historic emission equally, regardless of when it occurred, for less-developed countries[47] (with a population of 4.8 billion in 1999) was a mere 24% of the global total, compared with 76% for more-developed countries (with a population of 1.2 billion in 1999).[48] Recent research found that for the period 1980–2005, high-income nations had 7% of the world's population growth and 29% of the growth in CO_2 emissions. Furthermore, most of the nations with the highest population growth rates had low growth rates for CO_2 emissions, while many of the nations with the lowest population growth rates had high growth rates for CO_2 emissions.[49] In other words, the more-developed countries have a higher per capita CO_2 emission compared with the less-developed (see Figure 2.2). For instance, China's per capita CO_2 emission was 2.15 tons in 1990, rising to 2.69 tons in

---

46. The UN defines the 'more-developed countries' as all regions of Europe plus North America, Australia/New Zealand and Japan.
47. The UN defines the 'less-developed region' as all countries of Africa, Asia (excluding Japan), Latin America and the Caribbean plus Melanesia, Micronesia and Polynesia.
48. *Navigating the Numbers: Greenhouse Gas Data and International Climate Policy.* The data excludes emissions from land use.
49. Dr David Satterthwaite, *Environment and Urbanization*, September 2009.

2000 and 5.26 tons in 2008. Similarly, for India the figures are 0.8 tons per person per year in 1990, 1.14 tons in 2000 and 1.47 tons in 2008. The respective annual figures for the US are 19.14 tons, 19.15 tons and 17.5 tons; and those for the UK are 9.96 tons, 9.23 tonnes and 8.54 tons.[50]

Incensed by the implications of blaming population growth for our environmental degradation, some environmentalists have shifted the blame to the rich and wealthy. In a forthright response to James Lovelock's claim that environmental problems are inseparable from population growth, George Monbiot wrote:

'While there's a weak correlation between global warming and population growth, there's a strong correlation between global warming and wealth... It's time we had the guts to name the problem. It's not sex; it's money. It's not the poor; it's the rich.'[51]

He cites the observation by David Satterthwaite in the journal *Environment and Urbanization* that between 1980 and 2005, sub-Saharan Africa produced 18.5% of the world's population growth and just 2.4% of the growth in CO_2. North America turned out only 4% of the extra people, but 14% of the extra emissions, which is precisely why simply blaming the rich does not hold.[52]

---

50. United Nations, *The World at Six Billion*.
51. George Monbiot, *Guardian*, 28 September 2009.
52. *Techtalk*, Vol 52, No 23, MIT, 16 April 2008.

Consider, for instance, the US whose per capita footprint stands at 17.7 tons, four times the world average. If we assume that the richest 1% have a footprint 20 times the US national average (20 × 17.7 = 345 tons), then even if that figure is driven down to the national average of 17.7 tons, it would only result in a relatively small drop in the per capita footprint of the US as a whole to 14.3 tons, more than three times the world average. A study by Massachusetts Institute of Technology (MIT) students in 2007 found that: 'Regardless of income, there is a certain floor below which the individual carbon footprint of a person in the US will not drop.' The 'floor' below which nobody in the US can reach, no matter a person's energy choices, turned out to be 8.5 tons, almost twice the world average. That was the emission level calculated for a homeless person who ate in soup kitchens and slept in homeless shelters, and you can't get poorer than that.

Attacking the rich may be self-satisfying, but it does not provide a solution; it is a classic case of confronting the symptom and foregoing the disease. This is not to condone the wasteful extravagance of the rich; it is as repugnant as the fact that they should have so much money to burn in the first place; but that's capitalism. As far as the carbon footprint is concerned, the relevant distinction is not between rich and poor, but the more-developed and less-developed economies as we shall now show.

The level of CO_2 emission is determined by two factors, the size of the population and the per capita emissions (sometimes referred to as the average carbon footprint). If the population doubles and the per capita pollution is unchanged, the emission level will also double. Conversely, if population size drops by half, then emissions drop by the same ratio. Similarly, if the per capita emissions double while the size of the population remains the same, then emission levels will also double. And if both population and per capita emissions double, the emission level will quadruple. In general therefore:

$$\text{Emission level} = P \times P_k$$

where P is population and P_k is per capita emissions.

Let's look at each of these factors in turn, starting with population size. What causes a population to grow? The answer to this question is normally given by stating the obvious: a population increase occurs when the birth rate is higher than the death rate – this is known as 'the natural population increase'. In any given region, population growth rate depends on the natural increase and on migration. Global population growth however is determined exclusively by the natural increase. This raises the question 'what causes birth rates to rise and death rates to fall'?

Until recently, birth rates and death rates were about the same, keeping the population relatively stable: 0.31 billion in the year 1000, 0.5 billion in 1500, rising to just under 1 billion in 1800. However, this picture has changed dramatically since the Industrial Revolution and the birth of capitalism. While it took 800 years from 1000 to 1800 for the global population to increase by 0.67 billion, it has taken barely a quarter of that time to reach 7 billion – a sevenfold increase in just over 200 years.

The Industrial Revolution heralded another revolution, a revolution in science and technology, resulting in increases in food production and distribution, improvements in public health (water and sanitation), and medical technology (vaccines and antibiotics), along with gains in education and standards of living. It became possible to fight and cure diseases that were once fatal. Gradually, over a period of time, these discoveries and inventions spread throughout the world, lowering death rates and improving the quality of life for most people. The availability of antibiotics, immunisations, clean water and increased food production yielded tremendous improvements in infant and child mortality. Looking at the 20th century, the UN's *Population Challenges and Development Goals Report* puts it this way:

'During the twentieth century, mortality experienced the most rapid decline in the history of humanity. Although the sustained reduction of mortality had started in the eighteenth century, it gained momentum in the early part of the twentieth century as better hygiene, improved nutrition and medical practices based on scientific evidence became the rule in the more advanced countries. Despite the setbacks brought about by the First and Second World Wars, by the period 1950–1955, mortality had declined markedly in the more developed regions.

For example, by the middle of the twentieth century, average life expectancy had reached 66 years, ranging from 63 years in Southern Europe to 70 years in Australia and New Zealand.

The century also marked an important turning point in the less developed regions. With the expanded use of antibiotics, vaccines and insecticides, mortality in the developing world began to decline rapidly. For example, life expectancy for the less developed regions increased by slightly more than 50 per cent from 1950–1955 to 2000–2005, rising from about 41 to 63 years. As a result, the mortality differentials between the less developed and the more developed regions narrowed. By the period 2000–2005, the difference in life expectancy between the two groups amounted to 12 years instead of 25 years, the difference observed in the period 1950–1955.'

If one looks at the fertility rate, the number of children an average woman bears over her lifetime, a similar relationship with the prevailing socioeconomic order is observed (see Figure 2.3). In recent decades the low- to middle-income countries which have the world's highest birth rates have seen their fertility rate drop. According to the World Bank:

'The reasons for lower fertility are varied, but most are related to developing countries' economic growth and development. Parents choose to have smaller families when

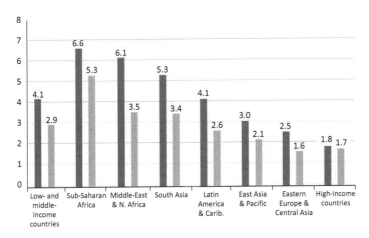

Source: World Bank

Figure 2.3 Average fertility rates, births per woman, 1980–99

health conditions improve because they no longer have to fear that many of their babies might die, and when they do not have to rely on their children to work on the family farm or business, or to take care of them in their old age. In addition, more parents are sending their daughters to school, which is important because women with basic education tend to produce healthier children and smaller families. More women now have opportunities to work outside the home, so they are starting their families later and having fewer children. On top of all that, access to modern contraceptives for family planning is improving, making it easier for parents to control the number and spacing of their children.'[53]

53. World Bank, *Why is World Population Growing Faster than Ever Before? When Will It Stabilise?*, 2004.

It is clear from the above that population size is closely related to the provision of healthcare, eradication of diseases, and the reduction in infant mortality, as well as more reliable food supplies, welfare, and general social amenities, factors that throughout history have always had a bearing on population.[54] For instance, the transition from the nomadic socioeconomic order of hunting and gathering to a new socioeconomic order of early human settlement, arable agriculture and animal husbandry made it possible to feed more people per square mile of land than could live in the same area before, thus stimulating population growth. More recently, giant strides in the fields of artificial fertilisers and medicine since the Industrial Revolution, and the birth of a new socioeconomic system of capitalism, brought about huge improvements in food production, a fall in infant and child mortality, the eradication of diseases and improvements in life expectancy. 'The bourgeoisie, historically, played a most revolutionary part' wrote Marx and Engels in 1848:

'The bourgeoisie, during its rule of scarce one hundred years, has created more massive and more colossal productive forces than have all preceding generations together. Subjection of

---

54. Writing about the effects of advances in science and technology, Steffen, et al, noted 'The Haber-Bosch synthesis revolutionised agriculture and sharply increased crop yields all over the world, which, together with vastly improved medical provisions, made possible the surge in human population', Will Steffen, et al, *The Anthropocene: Are Humans Now Overwhelming the Great Forces of Nature*, Royal Swedish Academy of Sciences, 2007.

*Nature's forces to man, machinery, application of chemistry to
industry and agriculture, steam-navigation, railways, electric
telegraphs, clearing of whole continents for cultivation,
canalisation of rivers, whole populations conjured out of the
ground – what earlier century had even a presentiment that
such productive forces slumbered in the lap of social labour?'*[55]

The second element that determines the level of CO_2
emissions, namely per capita emissions or average carbon
footprint, is even more directly related to the nature of the
socioeconomic order and its level of development. The carbon
footprint of the Middle Ages was miniscule compared with
that of the Industrial Revolution.

Within the same socioeconomic system, we find that the
level of development determines the level of CO_2 emission.
Today, with the capitalist system dominating the globe, we
see the more-developed regions emitting more CO_2 per capita
than the less-developed. The 2011 *United Nations Millennium
Development Goals Report* concludes that the:

*'[p]er capita emissions remain highest in the developed
regions – 11.2 metric tons of CO_2 per person per year in
2008, compared to about 2.9 metric tons in the developing
regions and 0.8 metric tons in sub-Saharan Africa, the lowest
regional value. The gap in CO_2 emissions per capita between
developed and developing regions has diminished somewhat*

---

55. *Communist Manifesto*, 1848.

since 1990: In 1990, 12.3 metric tons of CO_2 were emitted per person per year in developed regions, compared to about 1.7 metric tons in the developing regions and 0.9 metric tons in sub-Saharan Africa.[56]

Steffen, et al, referring to energy use as a major contributor to CO_2 emission estimated that 'industrial societies as a rule use four or five times as much energy as did agrarian ones, which in turn used three or four times as much energy as did hunting and gathering societies.'[57]

It follows from the above that neither the size of the population nor its rate of growth nor per capita emissions is an independent variable. Each of them is dependent, to one degree or another, on the type and level of prevailing development of the socioeconomic order.

Given that the level of emissions is a function of both the size of population (P) and per capita emissions (P_k), then: emission level = $P \times P_k$; and since both population size and per capita emissions are functions of the socioeconomic order, then emissions must also be a function of the socioeconomic order.[58] So statements such as the Earth is heading towards

---

56. *United Nations Millennium Development Goals Report*, 2011.
57. Will Steffen, et al, *The Anthropocene: Are Humans Now Overwhelming the Great Forces of Nature?* Royal Swedish Academy of Sciences, 2007.
58. If A is a function of B and B is a function of C, then A is a function of C. For example, given that improvements in health are a function of the availability of fresh vegetables, and that the availability of fresh vegetables is itself a function of thriving agriculture, then improvements in health are also a function of thriving agriculture.

irreversible changes in its climate as the developing nations increase per capita emissions to the same level as the developed world, should begin with the proviso 'given the capitalist system'. Such statements are predicated on a fundamental a priori assumption that the market economy will continue into the indefinite future – a capitalist mode of production motivated by the extraction of profit, a model that the developing countries seek to emulate or are in many cases forced to follow;[59] that capitalism is a constant, a permanent feature, that economic development is synonymous with commodity production, and that the market is the natural human condition – the natural order of things.

In times of crises, like the economic/financial and environmental crises facing humanity today, solutions are hindered by what John Kenneth Galbraith called 'conventional wisdom': 'ideas which are esteemed at any time for their acceptability ... and predictability.'[60] While Galbraith's conventional wisdoms of the 1970s, such as 'the importance of a balanced budget in times of crisis', are relatively easy to dislodge, the conventional wisdoms surrounding combating environmental degradation are of a different order of magnitude; they are more like dogmas than wisdom, not so

---

59. Naomi Klein, in her book *The Shock Doctrine*, cites numerous examples of countries forced to accept economic 'reforms' in return for loans from the IMF. 'The IMF had sneaked privatisation and "free trade" into Latin America and Africa under the cover of emergency "stabilisation" programs', p183.
60. JK Galbraith, *The Affluent Society*, Pelican, 1977, p36.

easily questioned let alone disowned.[61] It is so because there is more at stake. I refer here to the blind acceptance of the market as the natural order of things. The market is considered to be as natural to political economy as eating is to humans. Like eating, you may vary your diet and regulate your intake, but eat you must. So it is with the market, you may reform it and regulate it, but a market economy it remains.

While the 'excesses and failures' of the market are invariably identified (most incisively by Nicholas Stern in his review of the *Economics of Climate Change* (2006): 'Climate change is an example of market failure involving externalities and public goods... All in all, it must be regarded as market failure on the greatest scale the world has seen') the foundations upon which the market operates escape unscathed. As a consequence, solutions rarely go beyond attempts at regulation and modification of the way the market behaves, with concepts like 'prosperity without growth' which identifies economic growth as the culprit. Then there is 'opposing the tyranny of the bottom line', promoting a non-profiteering capitalist system, and 'internalisation of environmental costs', assigning a 'value' to free natural resources.[62]

Just as there is post-feudal society so must there be a post-capitalist economy. All the evidence points to the fact that, contrary to Fukuyama's 'end of history' thesis, evolution

---

61. 'In some measure the articulation of the conventional wisdom is a religious rite', JK Galbraith, *The Affluent Society*, Pelican, 1977, p38.
62. Detailed examination of these concepts is provided in Chapter 4.

continues and what at one time was considered to be rock solid, ultimately melts into insignificance. The post-capitalist economy beckons.

In the next two chapters we will take a look at the thinking behind the green agenda, the underlying theories and the proposals made, and ask if they are up to the task of halting environmental degradation and reversing climate change.

CHAPTER 3

The Illusions of 'New Economics'

The financial meltdown in October 2008 prompted the most immediate and radical responses from governments, politicians and economists. First the governments of the US and the UK came to the rescue with multi-billion bail-outs, not once, but several times. Then it was the turn of the media, who blamed the greedy, evil bankers and speculators with such headlines as 'Bank Crisis: End of the Road for the Dunces'[1] and 'Bring the Bankers to Account'.[2] Even testosterone-fuelled, male-dominated boardrooms were blamed for the crash.[3] Then there was the spectacle of the champions of neoliberal economics – the free-market gurus – falling on their swords

---

1. *Daily Mail*, 13 October 2008.
2. *Guardian*, 24 October 2008.
3. Matthew Hancock (former Chief of Staff to the Chancellor, George Osborne) and Nadhim Zahawi, *Masters of Nothing*, Kindle Edition, 9 September 2011.

in the manner of medieval knights who were ready to give their lives for the king. Alan Greenspan, the former US Federal Reserve Chairman, famous for his 18-year stewardship of US monetary policy, conceded in evidence to the US congressional committee that he was 'partially' wrong about deregulation, admitting that he 'had put too much faith in the self-correcting power of free markets' and that derivatives and credit default swaps had got out of control and needed to be restrained.[4] In other words, it's not a failure of capitalism, but a failure of regulation.

The mainstream environmentalists were not far behind. The slogan 'go green to save the planet' was promptly transformed to 'go green to save capitalism'. Capitalism was to save the planet through a new green revolution; now it is the new green revolution that is going to save capitalism.[5]

The theoretical backbone to the new green revolution is 'new economics', as championed by Herman Daly, Paul Hawken and others under such names as 'natural capitalism', the 'capitalism as if the world matters' of Jonathon Porritt, the 'natural economy' of Stuart Hart, the 'capitalism, but not as we know it' of Tim Jackson, or some other variant such as 'business for social responsibility' or 'social market economy'.

---

4. *New York Times*, 23 October 2008.
5. 22 October 2008, the United Nation's Environment Programme (UNEP) launched a 'Green Economy Initiative to get the global markets back to work', describing it as 'the best bet for real growth, combating climate change and triggering an employment boom in the 21st century'.

None of these concepts poses a challenge to the primacy of the market,[6] but will they bring about the transformation that is necessary to halt the degradation of the environment and reverse climate change?

NATURAL CAPITALISM

In their book *Natural Capitalism*, published in 2000, Paul Hawken, Amory Lovins and L Hunter Lovins begin with an image of the future: quiet cars and buses exuding water vapour, parks and greenways replacing urban freeways, low oil prices, dramatic improvements in living standards, etc. The authors ask if 'this is the vision of utopia?' The answer comes back, 'no': 'In fact the changes described here could come about in the decades to come as a result of economic and technological trends already in place.'[7] There is no argument that technological trends show that human ingenuity and resilience can indeed deliver what is asked of them. But 'economic trends', that's something the authors fail to substantiate apart from anecdotal evidence of this or that corporation embracing 'green' issues to make more profits. From the vantage point of 2012, the trends are in the opposite direction. Today, there

---

6. Jonathon Porritt, for instance, favourably quotes Tom Bentley in that capitalism 'now constitutes the only viable possibility of organising the economy', *Capitalism as if the World Matters*, Earthscan, 2007, p107.
7. Paul Hawken, Amory Lovins and L Hunter Lovins, *Natural Capitalism*, Back Bay Books, 2000, p2.

are more cars exuding ever more carbon into the atmosphere, more noise, and higher oil prices, with energy prices going through the roof.[8] The trend is higher unemployment, especially for the young,[9] and a concerted attack on standards of living as the UK and other governments attempt to rescue the economy from the severest crisis through relentless austerity programmes.[10] As for parks and greenways replacing urban freeways? Just look around you.

So, what is 'natural capitalism'? It's certainly not natural in the sense that it's God-given like the natural water we drink or the air we breathe. What the authors have in mind is a pristine capitalism, capitalism before it was corrupted by capitalists, an innocent capitalism, that has been abused. They believe that capitalism has no innate set of economic laws that govern its operation and that it was man who made the rules which have shaped capitalism, and had these sets of economic laws

---

8. '[Fuel] tariffs already rocketed 20% in the past year to an average £1,300', *Daily Mirror*, November 2011.

9. 'Youth unemployment has broken through the 1 million mark to a record high and the UK's wider unemployment rate has climbed to a 15-year high', *Independent on Sunday*, 16 October 2011.

10. 'Let's be blunt, 2011 is going to be a horrible year with cuts, job losses, price rises and pressure on pay and pensions, and thousands more ordinary working families will be pushed into the red as a result. Workers are facing an unprecedented assault on their living standards. Thanks to the increase in VAT, real wages this year are likely to be no higher than in 2005. It's clear these are hugely difficult times for working people', Frances O'Grady, TUC Deputy General Secretary, *Guardian*, 15 February 2011.

been different, capitalism could have developed and behaved differently. 'What if our economy were organised not around lifeless abstractions of neoclassical economics and accountancy but around the biological realities of nature?'[11] According to this theory, the 'lifeless abstractions' of supply and demand and marginal cost were imposed on the market by Adam Smith in the first case and Marshall in the second.

The authors even question the Generally Accepted Accounting Practice which treats natural and human resources as free amenities with inexhaustible supply and ask 'what if Generally Accepted Accounting Practice booked natural capital not as a free amenity in putative inexhaustible supply but as a finite and integrally valuable factor of production?'[12] But surely, isn't this what capitalists do? They consider natural resources as a 'finite and integrally valuable factor of production'. That is why they devote so much money and effort to capturing and extracting, and have easy access to these resources. Nations have been invaded, wars declared and hundreds of thousands killed and maimed just to lay a claim to the sources of such natural resources as oil fields, gold mines, forests, water and land. The very scramble for natural resources in Asia, Africa and Latin America by international corporations is a testimony to their recognition that these resources are 'finite and integrally valuable'. As for 'booking' these resources as a factor of production, the capitalists do that as well. For

---

11. Paul Hawken, et al, *Natural Capitalism*, Back Bay Books, 2000, p9.
12. Ibid.

instance, fossil fuel is purchased and booked in the same way as any other cost incurred in the process of production. Where these resources, such as air, don't have a price – where they are free – it makes no difference to the accounting practice whether they are 'booked' in the accounts or not, as we shall see presently.

Natural capitalism, say Paul Hawken, et al, 'recognises the critical interdependency between the production and use of human-made capital and the maintenance and supply of natural capital'.[13] By 'human-made capital' they mean 'manufactured capital including infrastructure, machines, tools and factories', and 'natural capital' 'includes all familiar resources used by mankind: water, minerals, oil, trees, fish, soil, air, etc'.[14] If natural capital is just the 'familiar resources', why call them capital? Just as 'a rose by any other name would smell as sweet', so 'familiar resources' by any other name have the same function. If we now replace the 'human-made capital' and 'natural capital' with the definitions Hawken, et al, give us, we find new capitalism (capitalism of a new type that is not so new after all): 'that recognises the critical interdependency between production and use of the infrastructure, machines, tools and factories and the maintenance and supply of familiar natural resources' – something that capitalism has always been aware of. It would be a very short-lived capitalist corporation that did not recognise the 'critical interdependency' of these

---

13. Ibid, pp3–4.
14. Ibid, p2.

three elements. It would be a very short-sighted and a not very successful capitalist who builds a factory in a place devoid of water (natural capital) with no adequately maintained transport (human-made capital).

CAPITAL

The authors are unhappy with what they call the 'traditional definition of capital' which they describe as the 'accumulated wealth in the form of investment, factories and equipment'. They assert that an economy 'needs four types of capital to function properly'.[15] The four types of capital they suggest are: human ('in the form of labour and intelligence, culture and organisation'), financial ('consisting of cash, investment and monetary instruments'), manufactured capital ('including infrastructure, machines, tools and factories') and natural ('made up of resources, living systems and ecosystems services'). Herman Daly, another promoter of natural capitalism, who describes himself as an ecological economist, 'broadens' the definition of capital:[16]

'Ecological economists have broadened the definition of capital to include the means of production provided by

---

15. Ibid, p4. This presumably means that capital can function with three or two or even one type of capital, albeit 'improperly'.
16. Herman Daly and Joshua Farley, *Ecological Economics Principles and Applications*, Island Press, 2004, p17.

nature. *We define capital as a stock that yields a flow of goods and services into the future. Stocks of manmade capital include our bodies and minds, the artefacts we create, and our social structures.'*

He goes on to define natural capital as:

'... a stock that yields a flow of natural services and tangible natural resources. This includes solar energy, land, minerals and fossil fuels, water, living organisms, and the services provided by the interaction of all these elements in ecological systems.'

Similarly, Jonathon Porritt defines capital without any reference to capitalism, the only reference is to 'humans':

'Capital is a stock of anything that has the capacity to generate a flow of benefits which are valued by humans.'[17]

While it is true that capital had existed before capitalism in the form of usurers' and commercial capital,[18] capital that begat the capitalist mode of production acquires a unique and

---

17. Jonathon Porritt, *Capitalism as if the World Matters*, Earthscan, 2007, p138.
18. 'Interest-bearing capital, or, as we may call it in its antiquated form, usurer's capital, belongs together with its twin brother, merchant's capital, to the antediluvian form of capital, which long precede the capitalist mode of production and are to be found in the most diverse economic formation of society', Karl Marx, *Capital*, Volume 3, Ch 36, p580.

different character – that of self-expansion, that of making a profit. To define capital without any reference to capitalism and its profit motive is like talking about Christ without mentioning Christianity. As for the types of capital, Jonathon Porritt prefers what he calls 'the Five Capitals Framework': natural, human, social, manufactured and financial.[19]

The underlying message is simple – capitalism is natural, and it is the natural order of things.

THE CENTRALITY OF THE MARKET

Paul Hawken, Jonathon Porritt and others agree on the centrality and desirability of the market. David Pearce, et al, extol the elegance and virtue of the free markets which economists have (generally) found attractive since the time of Adam Smith.[20] This is what Paul Hawken says:

'future economic progress can best take place in democratic, market-based systems of production and distribution.'[21]

They make a distinction between the old corrupt conventional capitalism – 'capitalism, as practised' – and natural capitalism. The former 'neglects to assign any value to the largest stock of capital it employs – the natural resources and living systems,

---

19. Jonathon Porritt, *Capitalism as if the World Matters*, Earthscan, 2007, p138.
20. DW Pearce, et al, *Blueprint for a Green Economy*, Earthscan, 1996, p154.
21. Paul Hawken, et al, *Natural Capitalism*, Back Bay Books, 2000, p9.

as well as the social and cultural systems that are the basis
of human capital'.[22] They argue that the practitioners of
capitalism, ie the capitalists themselves, have corrupted it.
It's harking back to Edward Heath's 'the unacceptable face of
capitalism' of the 1970s and anticipating the 'greedy, shameless
bankers and speculators' of 2008. They want capitalism to be
organised along what they consider to be its authentic rules.
They argue that since capital is a cost to business, then by
broadening the definition of capital to include free natural
resources, they present a cost to the capitalist just like other
costs such as raw materials, energy and rent. However, simply
calling something capital doesn't endow it with the properties
of capital, just as calling pigs 'birds' does not make them
fly. Even if 'natural capital' is 'booked' in the accounts, then
the cost assigned to it – since it is free – would be zero, and
nothing will change, as we shall see in the following chapter.

If the purpose behind the concept of natural capital is to
force business to take account of and pay for the damage done
to the environment, and thus provide business with incentives
to employ more environmentally friendly production
techniques, then it is unnecessary. It is unnecessary because
there is a time-honoured and universally applied method
of increasing the cost to business. It's called taxation. Local
councils' business rate and capital gains tax are just two
examples. Other taxes relate directly to the environment,
such as green taxes and the much talked about carbon tax and

22. Ibid, p5.

carbon emission trading. These are generally grouped under the heading of 'polluter pays'. However, the implications of the concept of natural capital go far beyond that. Natural capital turns nature into capital.

NATURE AS COMMODITY

The effect of categorising natural resources as capital is far more subtle than merely getting business to take account of the damage it does to the environment. The effect of designating natural resources as capital is that common public resources that are free today are given value. By giving free natural resources value – something that can only be expressed in terms of price, or what Adam Smith calls 'exchangeable value' – they become commodities. Solar energy, forests, air, water, green spaces, living organisms, the ecological system itself turn into commodities. And, like any other commodity, they can be bought and sold, traded on the commodity market and speculated upon. It opens the way for corporations to own rivers, open spaces and even the air we breathe. As capital, these natural resources can be used to make a profit like any other capital. Nature is thus transformed into private property, an exercise that has echoes of the land enclosures of the 16th century which launched the Industrial Revolution. Yet today it reflects not the vibrancy and energy of a new economic dawn, but the sluggishness of a decaying ageing organism.

WHAT IS CAPITAL?

Capitalism requires two distinct elements that complement each other: a capitalist with spare capital and a labourer who has nothing to sell but his labour power – a free-labourer.[23] Capital is money which, when put into a productive purpose, reproduces itself plus an extra amount that is called profit. Defining capital, Adam Smith wrote:

'When he [the capitalist] possesses stock sufficient to maintain him for months or years, he naturally endeavours to derive a revenue from the greater part of it; reserving only so much for his immediate consumption as may maintain him till this revenue begins to come in. His whole stock, therefore, is distinguished into two parts. That part which, he expects, is to afford him this revenue, is called his capital. The other is that which supplies his immediate consumption.'[24]

While business assets such as buildings and machinery are normally referred to as capital, they are in reality the particular

---

23. 'One thing, however, is clear – nature does not produce on the one side owners of money or commodities, and on the other men possessing nothing but their own labour-power. This relation has no natural basis, neither is its social basis one that is common to all historical periods. It is clearly the result of a past historical development, the product of many economical revolutions, of the extinction of a whole series of older forms of social production', Marx, *Capital*, Volume 1, Ch 4, para 7.
24. Adam Smith, *Wealth of Nations*, Book II, Ch I, para 2.

manifestation of money capital that is spent in the particular
capitalist enterprise. Consider a capitalist with a capital of
£100,000 to spend on a new business. Before he can start
trading, he acquires premises for £20,000, furniture, machines
and tools for £10,000, a wind turbine for £15,000 and raw
materials for a further £5,000 – a total of £50,000. His capital
remains £100,000 of which £50,000 are now in the form of
capital goods. Ultimately the whole of the capital is consumed
as trading begins in the form of wages, energy, rates, etc.

These forms that capital take are not different types of
capital as Paul Hawken and others suggest. They do not have
the attributes of capital, they are just different forms in which
money capital manifests itself. The fact that our capitalist
uses free natural resources such as sunlight and wind power
does not make his capital any larger. Only if these natural
resources which are now free are turned into commodities
to be purchased will the capitalist have to increase his capital
investment to cover these extra costs. Thus, describing free
natural resources as capital is 'a bad oxymoron' to use Herman
Daly's description of sustainable growth,[25] for that which is free
is not capital and that which is capital cannot be free.

Money becomes capital only in the process of production
through which capital acquires a unique property – that of
self-expansion. Money in an interest-bearing bank account
produces a return to its owner only because it is used in the

---

25. Herman Daly and Kenneth Townsend, *Valuing the Earth*, MIT Press, 1996,
    p267.

process of production by those who borrow from the bank. A hoard is not capital until it is invested or lent to someone to invest.

As such, capital is not unique to capitalism. There were commercial capital and usurers' capital in previous societies, but only under capitalism does capital acquire the property of self-expansion.[26] By investing £1000 in a capitalist business, the investor will receive back his investment together with an additional part, a profit. In the process, capital is converted into means and instruments of production, and commodities are produced and sold to reproduce the original capital plus profit.

In the context of capitalist production, capital is money that is spent to purchase such items and services as are required for the operation of the enterprise. The purchased items and services, be they raw materials, fuel, components, water, labour power, rent or waste disposal, are consumed by the process of production to produce a product that may then be sold. Also consumed in the process are natural resources and facilities such as air, solar energy and the environment in general, which, being freely available, the capitalist did not have to

---

26. Aristotle wrote 'that to derive interest from lending it out was to put it to an unnatural use' and that money is 'barren'. This is not because Aristotle was too stupid to realise that you can get interest on money, as Marshall contended, but because interest on money only makes sense in a capitalist system which creates surplus value, where money capital begets surplus, and as such has a price. In any other system, money, as Aristotle said, is 'barren'.

purchase. Once the product is sold, the money thus received from the sale covers not just the original advanced capital but also a certain amount of profit. A business, for instance that of making sausages, will require capital to cover expenditure on buildings, machinery, wages, fuel, water, electricity, rates and services such as waste disposal, as well as the meat and other ingredients used in the process of making sausages, ie things that generally come under the heading of instruments and means of production. In the process, freely available natural resources are consumed such as air for ventilation, oxygen to fire up the ovens, sunlight and so on. They are not commodities and as such have no price. They did not have to be purchased and thus do not figure as a cost to the business; they do not form part of the total capital expenditure on the business. If they are included in the accounts as suggested by Paul Hawken and others, then it would have a zero price which will change absolutely nothing in the accounts with no effect on the bottom line.[27] Only if these resources are privatised and converted into commodities in the same way as public assets are privatised, would these natural resources feature in a business account.

It is common to draw a flow diagram of a system to investigate how it works and understand its laws of motion. A typical flow diagram for an economic process is illustrated

---

27. A similar idea is advocated by the concept of the 'tyranny of the bottom line', the idea that what is wrong with capitalism is its insistence on making a profit. But if it didn't, it wouldn't be capitalism.

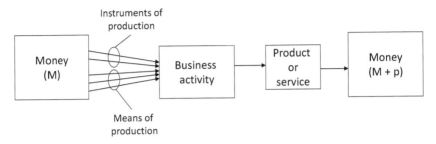

Figure 3.1 Flow diagram for an economic process

in Figure 3.1 in which, capital, an amount of money (M), is invested in a business which produces a product or provides a service that is subsequently sold.

Money (M) is used to purchase the necessary instruments and means of production for the business. Also used in the process are natural resources that are freely available such as sunlight, air, etc. The commodity produced in the form of a product or service is then sold for an amount of money that is larger than the original investment (M) by what is known as a return or a profit (p). The process also produces waste, some of which is disposed of properly, in which case the cost of disposal is included in the total expenditure as part of the means of production. Other waste, such as carbon emissions, is disposed of into the atmosphere at no additional cost.

In this system, all of the items that were purchased (the means of production and the instruments of production) together with the free natural resources are consumed by the business and disappear in their original form. The only thing that reappears in the same form as it was originally advanced is money, capital, except that at the end of the process there is more of it (M + p) than at the beginning (M). This is the distinguishing feature of capital. Unlike other goods, services and resources that were consumed, or partially consumed as in the case of buildings and machinery, only capital (M) is resurrected back to its original form but with a greater quantity, having been augmented with profit (p) of the very same kind, namely money, ready to enter the process all over again. It follows, therefore, that giving buildings, machinery, fuel, human skills, atmosphere and other natural resources the attributes of capital, as Paul Hawken and others do, is at best uninstructive.

It is argued that the closed system illustrated in Figure 3.1 is not a true representation of the economic process. Nicholas Georgescu-Roegen, for instance, insists that:

'Nothing could, therefore, be further from the truth than the notion that the economic process is an isolated, circular affair – as Marxist and standard analysis represent it, on the grounds that it ignores the 'natural environment.'[28]

He adds: 'From the viewpoint of thermodynamics, matter-energy enters the economic process in a state of low entropy and comes out of it in a state of high entropy,'[29] something

---

28. Herman Daly and Kenneth Townsend, *Valuing the Earth*, MIT Press, 1996, p81.
29. Ibid, pp76–7.

that is applicable to all systems by the very nature of entropy. He goes on to state that 'the notion [of entropy] is so involved' that 'it is not easily understood even by physicists,'[30] so what confidence can one have that he knows what he is talking about?

There are two main laws of thermodynamics. The first law, also known as the law of conservation of energy, states that energy can be changed from one form to another, but it cannot be created or destroyed. The second law deals with the effect of the transfer of energy on the availability of potential energy, what is known as entropy; the more entropy there is, the more disorder and hence less potential (or available) energy.

The second law of thermodynamics states that in all energy exchanges, in a closed system where no energy enters or leaves the system, the potential energy that can be transformed into useful work, will always be less than at the end of an exchange than at the beginning. For instance, when fossil fuel or wood is burned, or a battery is used, potential energy is consumed

---

30. Nicholas Georgescu-Roegen describes the laws of thermodynamics as 'peculiar', which is a very peculiar thing to say about a law of nature. The muddle is further compounded when Georgescu-Roegen refers to the 19th-century pioneer of thermodynamics, French engineer Sadi Carnot, who he says 'studied for the first time the economy of heat engines' and, confusing the meaning of economy as 'sparing or careful use' used by Carnot with economy as 'the wealth and resources of a community' used in economics, he concludes: 'Thermodynamics thus began as a physics of economic value and has remained so in spite of the numerous subsequent contributions of a more abstract nature.'

and transformed into useful work and, as a result, the total potential energy available is reduced; or, put another way, there is more entropy at the end than at the beginning. This is true for any system which transforms energy from one type to another, but it neither explains how a particular system works nor does it add anything to our understanding of it.

Take, for instance, an audio amplifier which transforms potential energy from the battery in the form of electricity into sound energy. Like all such systems, the total potential energy of the system is lower at the end than at the beginning. Or to use Nicholas Georgescu-Roegen's words: matter-energy enters the process in a state of low entropy and comes out of it in a state of high entropy. Having said that, we are no nearer to explaining how an amplifier works. To do so, we have to look into the laws governing electrical and electronic engineering, such as Ohm's law, amplification, modulation and electromagnetism.

The same applies to an economic system. Thus, statements such as '[f]rom a purely physical viewpoint, the economic process only transforms valuable natural resources (low entropy) into waste (high entropy)',[31] apart from being inaccurate, do not help us to understand how the system works. It is inaccurate in two senses. The first is that an economic system produces, in addition to 'waste', very physical commodities. Commodities such as an electric battery or tea

---

31. Herman Daly and Kenneth Townsend, *Valuing the Earth*, MIT Press, 1996, p80.

bags, which, being made of matter, contain high entropy. Furthermore, there is no such thing as 'waste', since, by the first law of thermodynamics, energy is never destroyed, only transformed. Therefore, the concept of waste 'from a purely physical viewpoint' does not exist. Waste exists only from the viewpoint of the economy.

Figure 3.2 shows a typical economic system in which natural environment considerations are included. This is known as an open system. On the input side, 'free natural resources' such as sunlight, air, etc, are introduced, and on the output side, waste discharged to the environment in the form of CO_2 emissions and other waste. It is evident that the additional input and output do not contribute anything new in relation to the way the economic process functions. Capital (M) is spent on the purchase of necessary items for the production process and none is spent on 'free natural resources', because they are free. Two products are produced: commodities and waste. The commodities in the

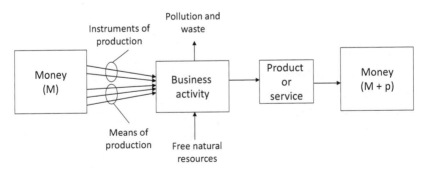

Figure 3.2 Open system, reproduces the flow diagram for a typical economic process taking account of the natural environment

form of products or services are sold and the original capital is augmented with profit (p). The waste is either disposed of properly, the cost of which is included in the total expenditure, or expelled into the atmosphere, rivers or soil.

But if the purpose of the exercise is to understand how the system works, the rules by which it operates, what makes it tick, then surely adding unnecessary elements to the flow diagram only serves to confuse and not to enlighten. In the same way as explaining the operation of an audio amplifier or an electric motor using a 'closed system' flow diagram, so it is with an economic process. Consider, for instance, an electric motor. It has a stationary coil called a stator which creates a magnetic field. When a current-carrying armature formed of looped wire is placed inside the magnetic field, the armature experiences a turning force proportional to the current in the wire and to the strength of the magnetic field which makes the armature rotate. The fact that in the process heat, noise, dust and smells are generated adds nothing to our understanding of what makes the electric motor turn. The heat, noise, dust and smell are merely unwanted by-products. To include them in the explanation of the laws underpinning the electric motor is unnecessary and confusing.

So it is with an economic process. It works according to its own internal laws, irrespective of any environmentally unfriendly by-products it may generate. The fact that a system spews pollution into the environment is not unimportant, but it is not part of the laws underpinning its operation. It is a by-product and not an active element in the process. Some of those who criticise the 'closed system' argue that the 'open system' brings into consideration the effect on the environment of the economic process; but if that is done at the expense of a proper understanding of the workings of the economic system, it will do only harm. For if the working of the economy is misunderstood, what hope is there of reforming it?

Those who fail to distinguish between the laws that underpin the operation of a system and its by-products do not only confuse the issue, but they also fail in the very task they set up for themselves, namely the creation of an environmentally friendly production system through (among other things) a more efficient use of energy. The only way to improve the efficiency of a system, be it a water pump, an internal combustion engine or a jet plane, is to fully understand its operation so that improvements can be made and new techniques introduced. The increased efficiency that we see taking place in electronic equipment such as computers, mobile phones and television receivers is achieved through full knowledge of the operation of these systems.

CHAPTER 4

Re-Claiming the Classicists: Adam Smith, David Ricardo and Karl Marx

The tsunami that hit the financial world in October 2008 came as a shock to the promoters of ecological economics like Herman Daly, Clive Hamilton and Richard Layard who believed Gordon Brown's assurance that he had ended boom-and-bust. Ironically, their no-growth, post-growth, steady-state society was predicated upon capitalism having moved to a new era of sustained uninterrupted growth. While 'Marxists called for the power of capital to be destroyed', Clive Hamilton 'calls for it to be ignored',[1] in the same manner that someone wishing to fly ignores gravity.

---

1. 'Whereas Marxism called for the power of capital to be destroyed, eudemonism [Hamilton's alternative programme] calls for it to be ignored. The possibility is permitted by the presence of abundance of democracy', Clive Hamilton, *Growth Fetish*, Pluto Press, 2002, p237.

While the classical economists attempted to enquire into the rules governing the capitalist mode of production, ecological economists preferred to impose their own rules on the economy. They believe that ideas determine how things work and develop, and that economic rules are not discovered through careful analysis but made up depending on one's moral and ethical standpoint. This is how Herman Daly deals with the role of labour in the determination of prices. He poses the question 'shall we conceive of labour as the only productive factor, the only source of value, and find that land and capital enhance the productivity of labour?'[2] His considered answer is: 'In a way, it all depends on how we want to look at it.'[3] This signals a retreat from the scientific analysis of the classical economists Adam Smith, David Ricardo and Karl Marx towards the subjective approach of Jeremy Bentham, John Stuart Mill and others.

Scientists often disagree on how to explain natural phenomena, such as the disagreement between Professor Higgs and Professor Hawking on the composition of 'dark matter' and the origin of mass. Such differences of opinion are sorted out through analysis based on observations. The Large Hadron Collider was built with that as one of its main objectives. It would be daft to suggest that 'it really depends on how you want to look at it'. Imagine for a moment that you are

2. Herman Daly, *Valuing the Earth*, MIT Press, 1996, p12.
3. Imagine Isaac Newton being asked if gravity is the only force pulling objects to the ground and answering 'it all depends on the way we want to look at it'.

confronted with two points of view about how sound travels: on one hand there is the particle theory and on the other the wave theory. Anyone who suggests that the true theory 'really depends on how you want to look at it' would be laughed out of court. Yet, when it comes to economics and economic phenomena, such an approach is taken seriously.

Herman Daly is not unique. Keynes, for instance, 'in his most famous observation, noted that we are ruled by ideas and by very little else'.[4] There are numerous others. In the 19th century, John Stuart Mill, acclaimed by Herman Daly as 'the great synthesiser of classical economics', in exploring the fundamental phenomenon of the capitalist mode of production, that of self-expansion and self-enrichment, wrote:

'I know not why it should be a matter of congratulation that persons who are already richer than anyone needs to be, should have doubled their means of consuming things which give little or no pleasure except as representatives of wealth; or that numbers of individuals should pass over, every year, from the middle classes into a richer class, or from the class of the occupied rich to that of the unoccupied. It is only in the backward countries of the world that increased production is still an important object: in those most advanced, what is economically needed is a better distribution, of which one indispensable means is a stricter restraint on population.'[5]

---

4. JK Galbraith, *The Affluent Society*, Pelican, 1977, p45.
5. JS Mill, *Principles of Political Economy*, Book IV, Ch 6, para 6.

Mill, surprisingly for such a prominent philosopher and economist, shows no inclination to enquire into this capitalist tendency of ever increasing profits.[6] Had he done so, he would have discovered that it, more than any other single feature, defines the capitalist system of production and exchange.

But economic laws do not disappear by simply ignoring them, they come and smack you in the face at times least expected. Like in October 2008. Blaming 'economic models' just won't do, for models are at best a reflection of the real thing, as is the case with modelling the weather system; changing the model does not change the weather, though it may get you more reliable weather forecasts depending on how accurate the model is. So it is with economics. There are laws that govern how the economy behaves and what makes it tick.

This chapter will argue that dismissing the foundations laid out by the classicists reduces political economy to the status of a faith modulated by moral values and personal preferences which may or may not be based on logic or fact. The chapter will go on to investigate the implications of one of the most contentious theories – Marx's theory of the tendency of the rate of profit to fall – showing that it provides a very consistent explanation of the financial and economic crisis that hit capitalism in 2008.

---

6. It's a good thing the legendary apple did not fall on Mill's head; it would have been wasted. Unlike Newton, who went on to discover gravity, Mill's response would undoubtedly have been along the lines: 'I know not why the apple should fall to the ground when it could move upwards or sideways;' and that would have been the end of the story.

Sources of value

Green economists like Herman Daly and Paul Hawken argue that economic laws are contrived by man and thus may be changed by man. There is no better illustration of this than in their treatment of the labour theory of value. This theory was first formulated by Adam Smith in *The Wealth of Nations*: 'Labour, therefore, is the real measure of the exchangeable value of all commodities.'[7] Adam Smith did not base this statement on abstract theorising or personal moral or ethical considerations. His work was firmly rooted in reality, the purpose of which was to understand how economics worked. He first observed that:

> *'The word VALUE, has two different meanings, and sometimes expresses the utility of some particular object, and sometimes the power of purchasing other goods which the possession of that object conveys. The one may be called "value in use", the other "value in exchange". The things which have the greatest value in use have frequently little or no value in exchange; and on the contrary, those which have the greatest value in exchange have frequently little or no value in use. Nothing is more useful than water: but it will purchase scarce anything; scarce anything can be had in exchange for it. A diamond, on the contrary, has scarce any value in use; but a very great quantity of other goods may frequently be had in exchange for it.'*

---

7. Adam Smith, *The Wealth of Nations*, Penguin, 1979, p133.

His examination of the price of commodities was thorough and methodical:

> *'In order to investigate the principles which regulate the exchangeable value of commodities, I shall endeavour to show, first, what is the real measure of this exchangeable value; or, wherein consists the real price of all commodities. Secondly, what are the different parts of which this real price is composed or made up? And, lastly, what are the different circumstances which sometimes raise some or all of these different parts of price above, and sometimes sink them below, their natural or ordinary rate; or, what are the causes which sometimes hinder the market price, that is, the actual price of commodities, from coinciding exactly with what may be called their natural price.'*[8]

Ecological economists abandon Adam Smith's scientific approach for something less concrete. After referring to the history of science, and citing examples of 'anomalies that brought crisis to old paradigms and were answered with new ones', such as 'shall we take the Sun or the Earth as the centre of the cosmos?' and 'are species fixed or slowly evolving?', Herman Daly poses a similar question for political economy, which he says 'may require more than normal puzzle solving':

---

8. Adam Smith, *The Wealth of Nations*, Penguin, 1979, p132.

'[S]hall we conceive of land, labour and capital as each being productive, and think in terms of three sources of value, or shall we conceive of labour as the only productive factor, the only source of value, and find that land and capital enhance the productivity of labour?' [9]

The distinction Herman Daly makes here is between land and capital as independent 'sources of value' that are as 'productive' as labour on one hand, and land and capital as subsidiary to labour and that merely 'enhance' the productivity of labour on the other.

Considering value, Smith, Ricardo and Marx make a distinction between two types of value: use value and exchange value. As Smith explained in the quote earlier, things which have the greatest value in use have frequently little or no value in exchange and vice versa. Land is indeed a source of value – use value, as indeed is labour.[10] However, land has no exchange value per se. It acquires an exchange value if, for instance, it is used for cultivation or for any productive purpose. A desert in the middle of the Sahara has no value whatsoever. However, if oil is discovered to be hidden underneath, it would suddenly become very valuable real estate. Labour, or to be more precise,

---

9. Herman Daly and Kenneth Townsend, *Valuing the Earth*, MIT Press, 1996, p12.

10. 'Labour is not the source of all wealth. Nature is just as much a source of use-value (and it is surely of such that material wealth consists!) as labour, which itself is only the manifestation of a force of nature, human labour power', Karl Marx, *Critique of the Gotha Programme*, Section I, para 2.

labour power, on one hand is not only a source of another value, but is also a source of exchange value as well. Capital, on the other hand, is money, the generalised form of wealth which may be used to purchase the use of labour and land (not to mention tools) and raw materials and other instruments and means of production. Capital is a source of use value, only to the extent that it can purchase sources of use value such as land, labour, tools and machinery, raw materials, etc.

As for land and capital being factors that 'enhance the productivity of labour', they are not unique; they do so in the same way as numerous other 'elements' such as water, the atmosphere, technology, tools of any kind, buildings and open spaces. Daly does not find it necessary to substantiate his view that capital and land are productive. He writes that such matters 'involve an element of faith, personal commitment and value' and, as such, 'are not reducible to logical or factual differences'.[11] Matters are not helped when he gives a different definition somewhere else. In the book that made ecological economics popular, Herman Daly defines capital as inclusive of land. This is what he says:

---

11. 'In a way it depends on how we want to look at it. And yet, there is far more to it than that. Which point of view is simpler or more appealing aesthetically? Which removes the intellectually or socially most vexing anomalies? Which is likely to suggest the most interesting and fruitful problems for future research? These kinds of criteria are not reducible to logical or factual differences. They involve a gestalt, an element of faith, personal commitment, and values', Herman Daly and Kenneth Townsend, *Valuing the Earth*, MIT Press, 1996, p12.

'Traditionally, economists have defined capital as produced means of production, where produced implies "produced by humans". Ecological economists have broadened the definition of capital to include the means of production provided by nature. We define capital as a stock that yields a flow of goods and services into the future. Stocks of manmade capital include our bodies and minds, the artefacts we create, and our social structures. Natural capital is a stock that yields a flow of natural services and tangible natural resources. This includes solar energy, land, minerals and fossil fuels, water, living organisms, and the services provided by the interaction of all these elements in ecological systems.' [12]

It is instructive how easy it is for some ecological economists to 'broaden the definition of capital' as if it is a matter of individual taste that needs no further explanation or investigation, let alone justification. Land, according to Daly's definition, is part of capital. Yet, in the passage from *Valuing the Earth*, quoted earlier, land is designated as one of three 'productive' factors, one of which is capital itself and one of 'three sources of value', one of which is capital.

THE LABOUR LAW OF VALUE

The labour theory of value is the central law of capitalism, without which no capitalist would be able to generate a

---

12. Herman Daly, *Ecological Economics*, p17.

profit. It was Adam Smith in *The Wealth of Nations* who first demonstrated that the quantity of labour time determines the exchange value of a commodity: 'Equal quantities of labour must at all times and in all places have the same value for the labourer.' The same law of value applies to the raw materials and means of production and they too have a value equal to the labour time expended in their production. Thus, the exchange value of a commodity is the sum total of labour time expended to produce it, including labour time expended past and present. 'As values, all commodities are only definite masses of congealed labour time.'[13]

Since Adam Smith considers labour as the absence of the labourer's 'rest, his freedom, and his happiness' – and that value is the same regardless of skill – then equal labour time must transfer an equal amount of value to the commodity. The problem with this formulation is how you explain the fact that skilled labour adds more value to a product than unskilled labour, when both are employed for the same amount of time. Furthermore, the theory as originally outlined by Adam Smith could not explain where profit comes from. Instead, capital is depicted as having a unique quality, a quality that yields profit, which begs the question: from whence does that quality come? He was followed by David Ricardo who went considerably further than Adam Smith, building on Smith's core premise that the value of commodities is determined by the quantity of labour embodied in them to derive a theory of profit. His

---

13. Marx, *Capital*, Volume 1, Ch 1, Section 1.

great advance over Adam Smith was to identify the division of the quantity of value added to the raw materials by labour into wages and profit. 'He shows that the value of commodities remains the same no matter what may be the proportion of these two parts.'[14] However, where Ricardo's theory falls is when it addresses the value of labour itself. This is how Marx explained it:

> *'But what is the value of a commodity? The objective form of the social labour expended in its production. And how do we measure the quantity of this value? By the quantity of the labour contained in it. How then is the value, e.g. of a 12 hours' working day, to be determined? By the 12 working hours contained in a working day of 12 hours, which is an absurd tautology.'*[15]

This sounded the death knell for the Ricardian School, to the obvious satisfaction of those who argued that profit is payment for 'abstinence'[16] from consumption or for risk taking by the capitalist, and of those who saw profit as a theft, fraud or simply cheating by the capitalist, buying under and selling over the value of the commodity.

---

14. Engels, Preface to *Capital*, Volume 2.
15. Marx, *Capital*, Volume 1, Ch 19, para 2.
16. 'I substitute for the word capital, considered as an instrument of production, the word abstinence', Nassau William Senior, *An Outline of the Science of Political Economy*, 1836.

It was Karl Marx who finally solved the riddle. The labour theory of value uses labour (or labour time) as the unit for measuring the value of a commodity. It follows that labour time, being the unit of measurement, cannot itself have any value.[17] To search for the value or price (which is the same thing) of labour time is like searching for the length of a metre or the weight of a kilogram, for both are units of measurement – the first of distance, and the second of mass. The only way the length of a metre or the mass of a kilogram can be described is in terms of another unit of measurement, such as inches and feet in one case and Imperial Pounds in the other.[18]

If labour has no value, then what does a worker offer in return for his or her wages?[19] What the worker offers an employer is not his labour or work, but his ability to labour or work – what Marx calls 'labour power':

'What economists therefore call value of labour, is in fact the value of labour-power, as it exists in the personality of the

---

17. 'Labour is the substance, and the immanent measure of value, but has itself no value', Marx, *Capital*, Volume 1, Ch 19, para 6.
18. The new SI system which defines the metre as equal to '1,650,763.73 wavelengths of the orange-red emission line in the electromagnetic spectrum of the krypton-86 atom in a vacuum' uses a specific wavelength as a unit of measurement.
19. 'That which comes directly face to face with the possessor of money on the market, is in fact not labour, but the labourer', *Capital*, Volume 1, Ch 19, para 6.

labourer, which is as different from its function, labour, as a machine is from the work it performs.'[20]

So, just as a machine has a value which is equal to the cost of its reproduction (the amount of labour required for its reproduction), so the value of 'labour power' is the cost of its reproduction; that is, the cost of keeping the labourer in a condition that he may continue to offer his labour power for sale – in other words, the worker's means of subsistence.[21] This is the reason why skilled workers attract a higher wage. It is because of the higher cost of their reproduction in terms of experience, education and training. To reproduce a highly skilled technician or doctor takes years of study and experience.

The precise value in money terms of the labouring power depends on a number of factors, including custom and practice, the relative strength of the working class and its trade unions, level of unemployment, and the state of the economy.[22] The basic unit cost of labour power is the unit

---

20. Marx, *Capital*, Volume 1, Ch 19, para 8.
21. Contrary to the opponents of Marx, subsistence does not mean impoverishment – its level depends on what Marx calls the level of civilisation in the country; the acceptable level of existence (*Capital*, Volume 1, Ch 22, para 10).
22. 'In contradistinction therefore to the case of other commodities, there enters into the determination of the value of labour-power a historical and moral element. Nevertheless, in a given country, at a given period, the average quantity of the means of subsistence necessary for the labourer is practically known', *Capital*, Volume 1, Ch 6, para 10.

cost of unskilled labour power.[23] In any specific period, say an
8-hour day, a skilled worker offers more units of labour power
than an unskilled worker and hence more value and more
surplus compared with a less skilled or unskilled labour force.[24]

When a worker is employed, he or she enters into a contract
which allows the employer to utilise the worker's labour power
for a number of hours, say a working day of 8 hours, or to
produce a number of items in an 8-hour working day, for
five days a week. In exchange, the worker gets paid the value
of his labour power in the form of a money wage. The value
added to the raw materials by the use of the labour power
is not the value of the labour power itself, but something
entirely different, namely the actual labour time spent by
the worker in meeting his or her part of the contract. The
difference between the value of labour power and the value
added to the raw materials by the endeavours of the worker is

---

23. Marx, *Capital*, Volume 1, Ch 1, para 28: 'Skilled labour counts only as
     simple labour intensified, or rather, as multiplied simple labour, a given
     quantity of skilled being considered equal to a greater quantity of simple
     labour.'
24. The value of a commodity would therefore remain constant, if the
     labour time required for its production also remained constant. But the
     latter changes with every variation in the productiveness of labour. This
     productiveness is determined by various circumstances including, amongst
     others, the average amount of skill of the workmen, the state of science, and
     the degree of its practical application, the social organisation of production,
     the extent and capabilities of the means of production, and by physical
     conditions (*Capital*, Volume 1, Part I, Ch 1, para 16).

the profit that the employer pockets as his own. For instance, if the contracted hours are 8 a day and the value of the labour power is the equivalent in labour-time terms of 6 hours work per day, then the difference (8 − 6 = 2 hours) is surplus labour constituting a profit for the employer. At all times and on average, equivalents are exchanged at their true values. There is no fraud involved and no cheating, and certainly no theft.

The surplus value that is produced by the exercise of labour power cannot all be pocketed by the immediate purchaser or capitalist. The latter has to share it with other capitalists who provide ancillary services that make it possible for the surplus value to be realised, such as advertising, transport, retail outlets, etc. They also purchase labour power, but they do not create surplus value; their profit comes from the surplus value created by the commodity-manufacturing capitalist whose share of the surplus value is thus reduced and becomes what is known as profit. On average, the division of the surplus value among the various capitalists is such as to equalise their rates of profit. The fluctuation and differences in the rate of profit of individual corporations, coupled with the movement of capital between corporations, are the means by which the overall rate of profit arrives at its average value.

THE RATE OF PROFIT AND ITS TENDENCY TO FALL

The tendency of the rate of profit to fall continues to haunt capitalism. Ever since it was confirmed as a fundamental law of capitalism by Karl Marx, huge efforts have been made to disprove it or at least to dismiss it as irrelevant. Karl Marx himself considered it as his most important contribution to political economy. So, what is it? A fundamental law of capitalism or just wishful thinking on the part of Karl Marx? Let's start by looking at profit, and how we measure its rate.

What on the surface seems a simple matter of dividing profit by invested capital to produce the rate of profit (RP) – RP = profit/capital investment – has become over the years a matter of contention. What figures for profit are to be used? Gross or net? Does investment include fixed capital? And what about interest on borrowed money? For our purposes, it does not make any difference which of the numerous definitions of profit is used provided we are consistent. The most basic representation of the rate of profit (and this is one used by Karl Marx) is the ratio of surplus value (s) made over a period of time divided by the capital consumed during the same period of time, taking account of turnover:

Rate of profit = surplus value/capital consumed

Capital consumed is the cost of raw materials, fuel, depreciation of machinery and buildings, tools and other equipment, rates, etc, which Marx calls constant capital (c), and wages, which Marx calls variable capital (v), for a specified period such as a year:

$$RP = s/(c + v)$$

where:

RP is the rate of profit
s is surplus value
c is constant capital (raw materials, etc)
v is variable capital (wages)

Capital consumed does not include the value of depreciated fixed capital, such as buildings, machinery, tools, etc, which may be used again. Fixed capital is not totally consumed and therefore only part of it, what is known as capital depreciation, is consumed, and that part enters the equation. The reason is obvious. If the fixed capital fully depreciates in 10 years (an annual depreciation rate of 10%), then a fixed capital of £1000 will depreciate by £100 each year – to £900 in the first year, £800 in the second, and so on until it depreciates to zero (and has to be replaced) in year 10.

What is the basis of the theory?

Given that the rate of profit $(RP) = s/(c + v)$, then, as capital accumulates, $(c + v)$ increases and the rate of profit decreases, provided surplus value does not increase by the same ratio. And here is why.

Assume c = £1000, v = £100 and s = £200. If the composition of capital changes in such a way as to double both c and v (from £1000 and £100 to £2000 and £200 respectively) and, as a consequence, surplus value increased from £200 to £300 (a 50% increase) then the rate of profit will change from:

$$RP1 = 200/(1000 + 100) = 18.2\%$$
to
$$RP2 = 300/(2000 + 200) = 13.6\%$$

If surplus value was doubled (an increase of 100%) to £400, then the rate of profit would remain the same, namely:

$$RP2' = 400/2200 = 18.2\%$$

And if surplus value more than doubled (an increase of say 120%, to £440), then the rate of profit will increase to:

$$RP2'' = 440/2200 = 20\%$$

To put it in terms of capital investment per worker (c/v) and surplus value per worker (s/v), the above formula may be rearranged as follows:

Given:

$$RP = s/(c + v)$$

then dividing the numerator and denominator by v, we get:

$$RP = (s/v)/(c/v + v/v)$$
$$= (s/v)/(c/v + 1)$$

Thus, as long as capital investment per worker (c/v) (or capital intensity[25]) increases more rapidly than does surplus value per worker (s/v), the rate of profit will fall. For instance, given a rate of profit of say 10%, then if capital intensity (c/v) is doubled (from 1 to 2), surplus per worker has to increase by 50% if the rate of profit is to remain unchanged. However, if c/v was to double from a higher base level, say from 20 to 40, then surplus per worker has to increase by 95% if the rate of profit is to remain unchanged. As capitalism develops it becomes less labour intensive, with increased use of capital equipment, the ratio c/v rises, s/v has to change by the same ratio as c/v if the rate of profit is to remain unchanged and the formula for the rate of profit is reduced to:

$$RP = (s/v)/(c/v)$$

As capital accumulation continues unabated (as it must under the capitalist mode of production), it becomes increasingly difficult to improve the rate of surplus value to maintain the rate of profit in the face of increasing capital intensity. If it ceases to be possible to increase the rate of surplus value fast enough, the rate of profit will fall. At some point, quantity changes into quality and the joints begin to fall apart. We shall see evidence of this with the 2008 financial and economic meltdown.

---

25. Marx calls this ratio the organic composition of capital.

The origins and treatment of the theory

Contrary to popular belief, the theory of the tendency of the rate of profit to fall did not originate with Marx. As Joseph Gillman explains:

'Recognition of the fact that the rate of profit tended to fall with the growth of the capitalist system was not original with Marx. It was a tenet of the classical economists before him. What was original with Marx was his explanation of the phenomenon, of its origin and its significance to the system. Adam Smith had treated the falling rate of profit at length some seventy five years before Marx... Except for Ricardo, the leading capitalist economists of the next century and a half followed Adam Smith's lead, as did also Malthus in Ricardo's day.'[26]

Ricardo, following Adam Smith, had also predicted a fall in the rate of profit only to dismiss it on the grounds that total profits would rise anyway:

'We should also expect that, however the rate of the profits of stock might diminish in consequence of the accumulation of capital on the land, and the rise of wages, yet that the aggregate amount of profits would increase.'[27]

26. Joseph M Gillman, *The Falling Rate of Profit*, Cameron Associates, 1958, pp1–2.
27. David Ricardo, *On the Principles of Political Economy and Taxation*, Cosimo, 2006, pp5–6.

Galbraith says the same thing:

'In this century, profits have shown no tendency to fall, and capital accumulation has continued apace. As a result, the declining rate of profit cannot be taken seriously as a cause of depression.' [28]

Karl Popper, explaining Marx's 'prophetic argument', confuses profit with the rate of profit in his much-regarded *The Open Society*, first published in 1945, in which he says: 'Marx believes that capitalist competition forces the capitalist's hand. It forces the capitalist to accumulate capital. By doing so, he works against his own long-term interests (since the accumulation of capital is liable to bring about a fall in his profits).' [29] Although Popper's work was republished several times since its first publication in 1945, this basic error was never acknowledged or corrected. Joan Robinson, amazingly for a Cambridge economist, also confuses profit with the rate of profit, ending the chapter on the falling rate of profit with: '… [Marx's] explanation of the falling tendency of profits explains nothing at all.' [30]

Chris Harman cites what Marx called 'counteracting influences' as a reason for the failure of the rate of profit to continue to fall over the last few decades:

---

28. JK Galbraith, *The Affluent Society*, Pelican, 1977, p87.
29. Karl Popper, *The Open Society*, Routledge Classics, 2003, Volume 2, p182.
30. Joan Robinson, *An Essay on Marxian Economics*, Macmillan, 1976, p42.

'If the "falling rate of profit" is an inexorable law, then it is difficult to see how capitalism has escaped from being in permanent crisis since the 1880s. It is true that Marx talked about "countervailing tendencies" which would counteract pressures towards crisis, but he hardly believed that these could prolong the rapid expansion of the system by more than a century.'[31]

Others blame 'leaks' of surplus value due to massive arms expenditure for the failure of the rate of profit to fall from the 1980s onwards, as if such expenditure falls outside the capitalist system: 'Each of these leaks [leaks of surplus value from a closed system] has acted to slow the rise in overall organic composition [of capital][32] and the fall in the rate of profit,'[33] says Kidron.

It is argued that the rate of profit falls only if Marx's rate of surplus value (s/v) remains constant. This is based on the following from Marx:

'If it is furthermore assumed that this gradual change in the composition of capital is not confined to some individual spheres of production, but occurs more or less in all, or at least in the most important ones, so that they imply changes in the organic average composition of the total capital of a certain

---

31. Chris Harman, *Explaining the Crisis*, Bookmarks, 1999, p19.
32. Marx uses 'organic composition of capital' as essentially the same as the ratio c/v.
33. Kidron, as quoted by Harman, *Explaining the Crisis*, Bookmarks, 1999, p39.

society, then the gradual and relative growth of the constant over the variable capital must necessarily lead to a gradual fall of the average rate of profit, so long as the rate of surplus-value, or the intensity of exploitation of labour by capital, remain the same.'[34]

However, Marx's statement 'so long as the rate of surplus-value … remain[s] the same' is a reference to a number of 'counteracting influences',[35] of which the rate of surplus value (s/v) is a major one.

There is nothing in the theory of the falling tendency of the rate of profit to suggest that the rate of surplus value must be constant. Regardless of what Marx wrote (or meant by what he wrote), the rate of profit will still fall even if the rate of surplus value increases, but with a smaller drop than would otherwise have been the case; how small depends on the increase in the rate of surplus value. As we shall now see, the relationship between the rate of profit and the rate of surplus value, far from refuting the theory that the rate of profit tends to fall, actually confirms it.

The falling tendency of the rate of profit could indeed be mitigated or even completely offset, by a rise in the rate of exploitation (s/v). This, of course, depends on the actual change in the rate of surplus value. If s/v does not rise enough compared with the increase in capital intensity (c/v), then

---

34. Marx, *Capital*, Volume 3, Ch 13, para 4.
35. Marx, *Capital*, Volume 3, Ch 14, Counteracting Causes.

the rate of profit (RP) will still fall. For instance, assuming s/v = 20% and c/v = 0.5 (50%), then RP = 13.3%. If capital intensity increases to 1.5 (150%), and the rate of surplus value remains constant at 20%, then the rate of profit drops to 8%.

With the same capital intensity of 1.5, the rate of profit would also drop if the rate of surplus value (s/v) went up to 30%. In this case, the rate of profit will drop to 12%, a drop of (13.3 – 12 =) 1.3 percentage points. Thus capital intensity (c/v) went up from 0.5 to 1.5 (an increase of 200%), the rate of surplus value (s/v) increased by 50% (from 20% to 30%) and the rate of profit dropped by 1.3 percentage points. Admittedly, the drop in the rate of profit is now smaller than that produced when the rate of surplus value remained at 20%, but it is a drop which satisfies the theory. The increase in the rate of surplus value is one of the factors cited by Karl Marx as a counteracting influence on the tendency of the rate of profit to fall.[36]

How the various elements, c/v and s/v, change depends on the scale and rate of development of the capitalist economy. In its infancy, a capitalist business is highly labour intensive, with a low ratio of capital to wages. As capitalism develops, more productive, labour-saving techniques are employed, with labour increasingly replaced by machines, and the ratio c/v begins to increase. This occurred most dramatically in the

---

36. '... opposite movements exert themselves, and that the tendency to reduce the rate of profit will be particularly checked by a raise in the rate of absolute surplus-value', Marx, *Capital*, Volume 3, Ch 14, para 6.

aftermath of the Industrial Revolution when thousands lost their jobs. This continues to be the case today. In the US, for instance, the ratio c/v increased by 32.6% in the period between 1947 and 2007.[37]

At the same time, the surplus extracted from each worker also increases, resulting in a higher rate of surplus value (s/v). However, while capital accumulation has no physical barrier, and thus c/v can continue to increase indefinitely, the same cannot be said of surplus value and the rate of surplus value. This is because there is a limit to both the length of the working day and the intensity of work (and with it a limit to the surplus produced) before the workforce is unable to regenerate itself. Thus, changes in the rate of surplus value cannot keep up with the unremitting increase in capital intensity and the rate of profit begins to drop.

But the theory stands or falls not on what Marx wrote and how it is interpreted but on empirical evidence of which we now have plenty.

THE DOG THAT DIDN'T BARK

While the rate of profit has clearly fallen over the last two or three centuries, in the last few decades, the phenomenon has

---

37. 'The reciprocal of the value composition (v/c) fell by 24.6% between 1947 and 2007', Andrew Kliman, *The Failure of Capitalist Production*, Pluto Press, 2011, p130. A fall of 24.6% of v/c is equal to an increase of 32.6% of c/v over the same period.

not been so clearly observed.[38] Since the 1970s, apart from the usual economic cyclic behaviour, the rate of profit in developing economies has to a large extent shown no tendency to fall.

It is this fact that convinced most Marxists to declare the theory of the falling rate of profit 'outdated', 'having no basis in fact' and 'with no value whatsoever'. It delighted its opponents who seized the opportunity to kill the theory off once and for all. Some sympathisers side-stepped, the implications, while others made magnificent efforts to show that while the theory was 'right in Marx's time' it is no longer applicable, or that the capitalists have managed to find a way around it; and yet others have contended that Marx's 'tendency' of the rate of profit to fall was not an empirical trend.

There is no reason to apologise for the theory, find a way around it or claim that it never meant what it was said to mean. There is a good reason why falling rates of profit have not been observed recently in developing economies. Rates of profit would gradually fall until they hit a 'critical threshold level', which, if crossed, would make the system collapse – in

---

38. Andrew Kliman in his paper *The Persistent Fall in Profitability Underlying the Current Crisis* concluded that 'US corporations' rate of profit began to fall about a decade after the end of World War II and the falling trend has persisted until the present time. Some measures of the rate of profit levelled off or increased very slightly after the early 1980s, while others have continued to decline. None indicates that a genuine, sustainable rebound in profitability took place.'

the same way as continuously reducing the idling speed of a car engine, below a certain critical threshold, would cause the engine to stall, or a drop in the human heart beat rate below 25 or 30 beats per minute (its critical threshold) will result in catastrophic heart failure. In the same way as a car engine cannot be observed running at a speed below its critical threshold (or a heart beating at a lower rate than its threshold of about 30 beats per minute), so a rate of profit lower than its critical threshold cannot be observed. If such a threshold was to be breached for any length of time, the system would suffer catastrophic failure.

Thus, empirical evidence would not show a rate of profit continuously falling below this critical threshold, in just the same way as the speed of an idling engine (or heart beat) cannot be observed or measured below their critical threshold. Once the rate of profit falls below that critical threshold, it has to be urgently rescued, otherwise, like our car engine and our human heart, the capitalist system would stall.

To circumvent this, capitalism must take any necessary measures, without much regard for people's jobs or living standards, to lift the rate of profit (and with it profits) above the critical level until the next time, and so on. Accordingly, the rate of profit fluctuates around the threshold level but does not consistently fall. From this point of view, capitalism digs its own grave.[39] The real crisis occurs not when the rate of profit

---

39. 'What the bourgeoisie therefore produces, above all, are its own grave-diggers', Marx and Engels, *Communist Manifesto*.

falls but when it stops falling, because it only stops falling when it is teetering at the threshold of total collapse.

To observe the phenomenon of the falling tendency of the rate of profit, therefore, we need to borrow a technique frequently used in science and technology.

In science, where a phenomenon such as temperature or the movement of an electron cannot be observed directly, an indirect approach is used. The simple mercury thermometer, for instance, does not measure temperature directly. What is observed is the effect a change in temperature has on mercury consigned to a narrow tube; it expands and that expansion is a measure of a change in temperature. Similarly, having found that a moving electron creates a magnetic field, the presence of the latter is then used to detect the presence of moving electrons in a conductor. So it is with the theory of the tendency of the rate of profit to fall. If we can ascertain the repercussions of a falling rate of profit, then if they are observed in the economy, we can safely conclude that the theory is correct.

THEORETICAL IMPLICATIONS OF A FALLING RATE OF PROFIT

By itself, a fall in the rate of profit is of little consequence to an individual capitalist so long as profits continually increase. This is why Adam Smith, David Ricardo and others dismissed it as irrelevant. Karl Popper puts it this way:

'The situation for a successful average capitalist, will be this: he sees his income rise quickly, and his capital still more quickly; that is to say, his savings rise more quickly than the part of his income which he consumes. I do not think that this is a situation which must force him to desperate measures, or which makes a compromise with the workers impossible.'[40]

It is of course true. A fall in the rate of profit does not necessarily result in a drop in profits. Changes in overall profits depend on the quantity of capital investment as well as on the rate of profit. Thus, if over a period of time the rate of profit falls by half, say from 10% to 5%, and at the same time total investment is doubled, from say £100,0000 to £200,000, profits accrued will not change: 10% of £100,000 is the same as 5% of £200,000. In both scenarios, we end up with a profit of £10,000. If, on the other hand, as a result of technical improvements, capital investment increased by more than double, profits would go up in spite of the 50% drop in the rate of profit. Conversely, if the increase in capital investment is less than double, profits will fall. In general, if the rate of capital accumulation is less than the rate of the fall in the rate of profit (ie the percentage increase in capital invested is less than the fall in the rate of profit expressed as a percentage), then profits will begin to drop.

---

40. Karl Popper, *The Open Society*, Volume 2, Routledge, 2003, p202.

In a boom, profits are high and capital accumulates, yielding even more profits. However, if for any reason the rate of profit falls, then in order to maintain the overall profit level, investment must be increased to counterbalance the fall in the rate of profit. This goes on until a critical threshold is reached, at which point the additional investment necessary to maintain the overall profit level is higher than the market can provide. Profits can be prevented from falling either by transferring money from the public sector (or the public at large) to the profit-making sector, or by increasing the circulation of the available capital to make the same capital work harder, so to speak, or both.

The amount of additional investment necessary to compensate for a fall in the rate of profit will depend on the baseline investment. An initial capital of £10 million invested at an annual rate of profit of 5% would yield a profit of £500,000. If the rate of profit fell by 20%, to 4%, profit would drop to £400,000. To compensate for this drop, investment must go up to £12.5 million, a rise of £2.5 million – a relatively small amount which may not be too excessive for the market to provide. However, if the baseline investment was £10 billion instead of £10 million, then the additional investment necessary to maintain profits for the same drop in the rate of profit would be 1000 times greater, at £2500 million. If the rate of profit fell by more than 1%, an even greater additional investment would be necessary.

In highly developed economies such as those of the US and the UK, in which the baseline capital investment is measured in trillions, even a modest drop in the rate of profit would necessitate additional investment in billions if profits were to be maintained. In general, as capitalism develops and capital accumulates, the baseline investment increases and with it the level of additional investment necessary to counteract a fall in the rate of profit. Eventually a tipping point will be reached at which the necessary increase in investment to counterbalance a drop in the rate of profit will be prohibitively high – greater than the market can provide.

THE OPERATING MAP OF CAPITAL

The traditional time series is a useful tool that has formed the backbone of almost all economic analysis. But the time series has severe limitations. While it shows how individual items, say profit, prices or unemployment, vary over time, it is limited to only one variable at any one time. Our investigation involves the relationship between three variables: the quantity of capital investment, the rate of profit and time. To effect this investigation, we will make use of a technique widely utilised in science and engineering of which the operating characteristic curve of the simple transistor is just one example.

We will start with a graph of the rate of profit against capital investment – what I will call the characteristic curve – to show how the rate of profit changes as capital accumulates. Assuming the theory of the falling rate of profit is correct, we will get a curve sloping downwards as capital accumulates and the rate of profit falls over time as shown in Figure 4.1.

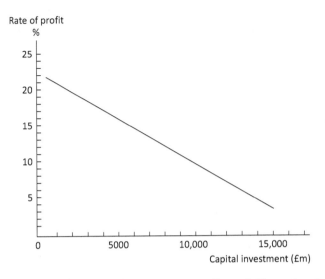

Figure 4.1 A straight-line trajectory representing a falling rate of profit as capital accumulates

A straight-line trajectory is used merely for illustrative purposes. In the real economy, of course, the operating curve would not be a straight line, but would fluctuate above and below the downward trajectory. It may even go backwards. But if the theory is correct, over a period of time as capital investment increases, the trajectory will nonetheless be moving downwards.

Using the same axes, a curve representing the rate of profit returned by a constant level of profit for different values of capital investment may be drawn.[41] For different values of

41. This is a hyperbola with the mathematical expression of profit divided by capital investment ($f = p/x$).

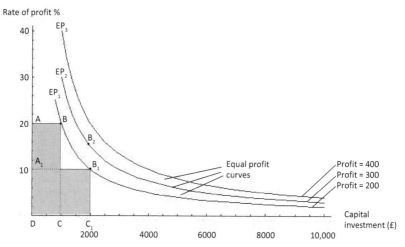

Figure 4.2 Equal profit (EP) contours

profit we get a set of these curves, which I will call the equal profit (EP) curves or contours as shown in Figure 4.2.

Consider point B on the equal profit contour EP_1. The area under point B represents the profit obtained by capital operating at this point (the rate of profit multiplied by the investment), namely area ABCD = DA × DC = 20% × £1000 = £200. Similarly for point B_1 on the same contour EP_1, profit = area $A_1B_1C_1D$ = 10% × £2000 = £200. The same applies to any other point on that contour. EP_1 is, therefore, a £200-profit contour. In the same way, points on the other two contours represent other profit levels, namely £300 for EP_2 and £400 for EP_3. If the operating point moves 'upwards', from EP_1 to EP_2 or from EP_2 to EP_3, profits will increase and vice versa.

If we now superimpose the first graph over an expanded version of the second, we get a graph showing the relationship between three variables: rate of profit, profit, and capital investment – the operating map of capital (what I will call the economic footprint).

In Figure 4.3, points P_1, P_2, P_3, etc, are the operating points of capital at equal time intervals (the duration of which need not necessarily be one year). It can be seen that as capital accumulates, and rate of profit falls, the operating point first crosses the EP contours upwards, from a low to a high EP contour (P_1 to P_2, P_2 to P_3, P_3 to P_4, P_4 to P_5 and P_5 to P_6). Each time, profits go up. After P_6, the operating point moves to P_7 on the same EP contour and profits are unchanged. Any further fall in the rate of profit (from P_7 to P_8) and profits start to tumble as the operating point begins to move from a high to a low EP contour.

It will also be noticed that although the gradient of the characteristic curve (ie the rate of change in the rate of profit

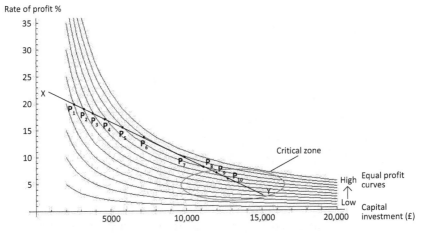

Figure 4.3 Notional evolution of the operating map of capital

as investment increases) is the same throughout, the operating curve crosses the EP contours upwards at low levels of capital accumulation and downwards at high levels of accumulation. This is because as capital accumulates, an increasingly large quantity of capital investment is necessary to compensate for any given drop in the rate of profit and to ensure the same overall profit. As capital accumulation continues apace, a critical point is reached (P_8 in the diagram) when capital cannot accumulate fast enough to compensate for the drop in the rate of profit.[42] Profits begin to fall. This is the critical zone,[43] as opposed to the conventional or classical zone when capital operated in the high EP contours.

As far as our illustration is concerned, the rate of profit will continue to fall, dragging overall profits down with it. However, this cannot be allowed to happen as this will signal the end of capitalism. Action must therefore be taken to push the rate of profit back up above its critical threshold. As stated earlier, the straight-line characteristic curve is used for illustrative purposes only. In a real economy, the characteristic curve will fluctuate above and below a trajectory, which, if the theory of the falling rate of profit is correct, will have a downward gradient. Regardless of the path that a real-economy

---

42. 'Through its own development, [capitalism] drives towards the point at which it makes itself impossible', Engels, *Anti-Duhring*, Foreign Language Publishing House, Moscow, 1962, p171.
43. 'Thus the law [of the falling rate of profit] acts only as a tendency. And it is only under certain circumstances and after long periods that its effects become strikingly pronounced', Marx, *Capital*, Volume 3, Ch 14, para 18.

characteristic curve takes as it zig-zags along, if it starts at P_1 and ends at P_{10}, then it must cross the EP curves downwards at least once. In other words, it must enter the critical zone sometime along the way.

It follows from the above that if the rate of profit does have a tendency to fall, then one would expect on one hand that the economy would move towards a critical zone in which incremental increases in capital investment lead to a fall in profit below its critical threshold and, on the other hand, that once the economy comes out of the critical zone, its rate of profit would climb up to its pre-critical-zone level. Crossing of the EP contours downwards is not by itself evidence of the critical zone. The characteristic curves of economic downturns and recessions invariably cross the EP curves downwards as profits fall. However, that does not necessarily mean that the economy is in the critical zone. This is because an economy enters the critical zone only when it is operating at the flat end of the EP curves. The critical zone is the coincidence of two things: high capital accumulation and a low rate of profit, both of which are relative quantities; yet, given a certain combination in any economy, they form an absolute threshold.

To prevent the economy diving into the critical zone, action must be taken to, on one hand, maintain the rate of profit above its critical threshold and, on the other, ensure an increasingly large supply of capital investment going to the profit-making sector.

If we now look at the operating map of real economies, and if they exhibit similar features in terms of critical thresholds and critical zones, this would substantiate the theory of the falling rate of profit and go a long way towards explaining the uniqueness of the economic crises of the 1970s onwards. Let's look at the UK economy of 1965–79.

Figure 4.4 shows the economic footprint of the UK private non-financial sector in 1965–79.[44] It shows total capital outlay

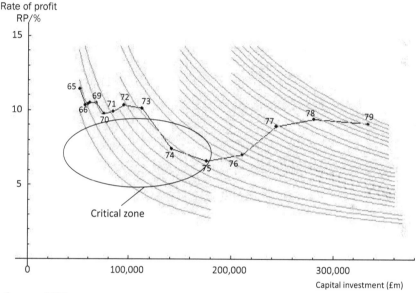

Source: ONS

Figure 4.4 UK economic footprint (private non-financial corporations) 1965–79, gross

44. Source: Office for National Statistics, private non-financial corporations (PNFC), UK, 1965–79. The non-financial sector is chosen as it is the sector where surplus value is created forming the backbone of the real economy. The figures are not price-index adjusted. If they were, the characteristic curve would follow a similar course, exhibiting 'clusters' where capital shrinkage takes place.

continuously increasing year on year. Throughout 1965–73, the increase in capital investment was always enough to ensure increased profits as indicated by the operating curve crossing the EP contours upwards. This took place regardless of the fact that in 1965–66, 1969–70 and 1972–73 the rate of profit actually fell (Table 4.1).[45]

In each case where there was a drop in the rate of profit, the increase in capital investment was proportionately higher than the drop in the rate of profit, thus ensuring increased profits: a 10.2% increase in investment compared with a 9.6% drop in the rate of profit (1965–66), an 11.7% increase compared with a 7.6% drop (1969–70) and an 18.5% increase compared with a 1.0% drop (1972–73).

In 1973–74, things took an unexpected turn. Although capital investment rose by an unprecedented £28.8 billion (25.6%), it was not enough to compensate for the 27.5% drop in the rate of profit. Profits tumbled as the characteristic curve crossed the critical zone threshold. Capitalism – production for profit – was under threat. Capitalism was perched at the edge of a vortex. It was this that made the crisis of 1973–74 so unique. The 'party' was well and truly over.[46] The following year, the rate of profit dropped again (9.5%) but the increase

---

45. The figures for investment are not inflation adjusted. If price adjustment was introduced, capital retrenchment would have been observed (see Appendix).
46. Anthony Crosland, the Labour Secretary of State for the Environment in 1974, told Local Authority representatives 'the party's over'.

Table 4.1 Capital investment (column 2) year on year, and its corresponding rate of profit (column 5) for private non-financial corporations (PNFCs) in the UK

	Capital £m	Capital change £m	Capital % change	Rate of profit %	Rate of profit % change
1965	51,184			11.4	
1966	56,406	5222	10.2	10.3	9.6
1967	58,463	2057	3.6	10.4	−1.0
1968	61,338	2875	4.9	10.5	−1.0
1969	67,080	5742	9.4	10.5	0.0
1970	74,951	7871	11.7	9.7	7.6
1971	84,266	9315	12.4	10.0	−3.1
1972	95,239	10,973	13.0	10.3	−3.0
1973	112,858	17,619	18.5	10.2	1.0
1974	141,701	28,843	25.6	7.4	27.5
1975	175,992	34,291	24.2	6.7	9.5
1976	210,156	34,164	19.4	7.0	−4.5
1977	243,476	33,320	15.9	9.0	−28.6
1978	280,634	37,158	15.3	9.5	−5.6
1979	363,266	82,632	29.4	9.2	3.2

in capital investment was high enough (£34.3 billion or 24.2%) to ensure increased profits.

For the UK economy of 1965–79 the movement of the operating point is what the theory predicted.[47] For the theory to be fully vindicated, more than one economy has to display the same characteristics, which is something that is beyond the scope of this book to fully explore. (More footprints for the UK and the US economies are included in the Appendix.)

---

47. A similar phenomenon is observed when the characteristic curve of other economies, the US in particular, are constructed, as illustrated in the Appendix.

Furthermore, as demonstrated earlier, if the theory is correct then once the economy breaches its critical threshold measures are taken to ensure its return to its previous level. A look at the operating map for the UK economy of 1965–2010 confirms this.

But first, let's briefly consider the immediate consequences of an economy breaching the critical zone threshold. When the economy hits the critical zone, profits begin to decline. The economy has two options: either expand capital outlay by increased investment to improve profits (the very response that brought the economy to this point in the first place), or cut out investment in the least profitable lines of production to improve the average rate of profit on the remaining capital – a process that takes time to produce results. Discarding marginal investment reduces total capital outlay, which, given a rate of profit that has yet to improve, results in reducing profits further which leads to the further discarding of marginal investment and so on in a downward cycle. The very opposite of what is required to move out of the critical zone actually takes place. Discarding marginal investment takes the form of closures and bankruptcy of those firms that are most exposed.

The UK economic footprint for 1965–2010 for private non-financial corporations is shown in Figure 4.5. As predicted by the theory, the rate of profit recovered from its dip in 1974–75. Although the recovery was remarkably swift, the episode nonetheless gave a serious jolt to governments and corporations, ushering in a new economic and political climate that has defined the UK ever since – a climate

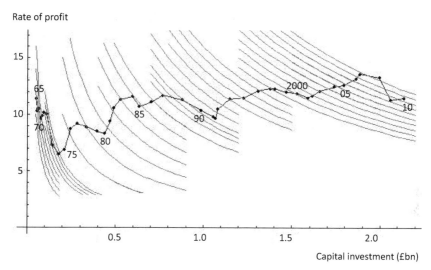

Source: ONS

Figure 4.5 UK economic footprint (private non-financial corporations) 1965–2010

marked at various stages by a squeeze on pay and conditions, privatisation, anti-trade-union legislation, deregulation and the Private Finance Initiative (PFI).[48]

Keynesian economics was abandoned in the second half of the 1970s when it was found that it no longer provided the solution to capitalism diving into the critical zone, at a time when profits were tumbling as capital investment could not

---

48. 'While individual countries may have at least one horror story of radical marketisation similar to Britain's, only Britain can tell them all. The process has gone further and faster here', Will Hutton, *The State We're In*, Vintage, 1995, p18.

keep up with a falling rate of profit. The Middle East war in 1973 and the subsequent formation of OPEC did contribute to the ensuing crisis; however, as Larry Elliott and Dan Atkinson noted in *The Age of Insecurity*, these events 'hastened the demise of the post-war system, it would have died anyway, but a longer slower death'.[49]

There was an urgent need to increase the size of profit-making capital on one hand and reduce wages on the other. It was Labour's Prime Minister James Callaghan who announced the end of Keynesian economics at the Labour Party Conference at the height of the IMF crisis in 1976:[50] 'Callaghan provided the overture for Thatcherism, pioneering many of her themes.'[51] His government (of 1976–79) took measures to deal with the wage front, introducing a wage freeze and drastic cuts in public services. The Winter of Discontent followed with mass strikes against government-sponsored wage restraint.

49. Larry Elliott and Dan Atkinson, *The Age of Insecurity*, Verso, 1999, p53.
50. 'The cosy world we were told would go on forever, where full-employment would be guaranteed by a stroke of the Chancellor's pen, cutting taxes, deficit spending – that sort of cosy world is gone... We used to think that we could spend our way out of recession and increase employment by cutting taxes and increasing government spending. I tell you in all candour that that option no longer exists, and in so far as it ever existed, it only worked on each occasion since the war by injecting a bigger dose of inflation in the economy, followed by a higher level of unemployment at the next step', from James Callaghan's speech to the Labour Party Conference, 1967.
51. Larry Elliott and Dan Atkinson, *The Age of Insecurity*, Verso, 1999, p53.

The Tory government under Thatcher consolidated what the previous government started with a twin-pronged strategy: comprehensive deregulation of capitalist corporations on one hand and strict regulation of trade unions on the other. The wholesale privatisation of nationalised industries and public utilities transferred extraordinary amounts of capital from the non-profit-making public sector to the profit-making private sector. In the 1980s and 1990s we witnessed the biggest-ever rise in personal debt, a fast growth in inequality, a move away from manufacturing, an aggressive privatisation programme,[52] a comprehensive attack on the welfare state, massive deregulation of the finance system and an all-encompassing assault on trade unions, coupled with changes in the taxation system that favoured the rich and the wealthy.

Under the stewardship of New Labour (1997–2010) a more pernicious form of privatisation was introduced in places where the previous Tory government had dared not go. Introduced by the then Conservative government in 1992, the Private Finance Initiative (PFI) was vitalised and re-branded as Public–Private Partnership (PPP), an umbrella term that includes PFI. The Private Finance Initiative, which did not get off the ground under the Conservative government because it refused to make enough concessions to the private sector, was pursued with vigour by the Labour government. 'In 1997,

---

52. 'In the 1980s, a total of £60 billion of state assets were sold at knock-down prices to the private sector', Ankie Hoogvelt, *Globalization and the Postcolonial World*, Palgrave, 2001, p152.

the incoming Labour government resuscitated the policy
and got PFI projects off the ground. It removed a number of
obstacles and introduced legislation'[53] to entice bidders and
their financial backers. Up to 1997, a mere 17 PFI contracts
had been signed to the value of £2.95 billion. From 1997 to
2007, there were 550 PPP contracts signed, with a total capital
of £51 billion.[54]

As a result of the actions taken by successive governments,
the UK economic footprint climbed up and began to cross
the EP contours upwards, and continued to do so (with the
exceptions of 1984–85) until 2008–09 when once again it
dipped below its critical threshold and began to cross the EP
contours downwards, ushering in the deepest financial and
economic crisis capitalism has ever had.[55] The banking system
was on the verge of collapse for lack of capital and had to be
rescued with a multi-billion pound bail-out. When that proved
inadequate, the Bank of England started printing money –
what they prefer to call quantitative easing. The government,
meanwhile, responded with an all-encompassing austerity
programme designed to transfer further capital to the profit-
making sector of the economy through a programme of cuts in
welfare, pensions and education spending, as well as reduction

53. Ken Coghill and Dennis Woodward, *The Challenge of Public-Private
    Partnership*, Edward Elgar, 2005, pp191–2.
54. Office for National Statistics.
55. 'This is undoubtedly the biggest financial crisis the world has ever faced',
    Mervyn King, Governor of the Bank of England speaking on *Channel 4
    News*, October 2011.

in local council grants and a rise in university tuition fees to pledge the future earnings of thousands of graduates to the banks.

Figure 4.6 shows the turmoil that successive governments have had to inflict on the British people to lift capital out of the critical zone in the years following the crisis of 1973–74.

Privatisation alone transferred over £60 billion from the non-profit economy to the private sector.[56] This was accompanied later by the Labour government's Public–Private Partnership (the name it gave to PFI) which ensured a high rate of return for investments at the expense of the taxpayer.

Further capital was conjured up through high levels of personal and government debt fuelled by, among other things, rising house prices and easier credit, dodgy financial packages and dealings that deregulation made possible, and real-time transborder circulation of capital; something that is facilitated by computer data processing and the internet. Debts of government and individuals went through the roof with the very worst instance being the growth of sub-prime mortgages.

CAPITALISM AT THE EDGE OF A VORTEX

Once it reaches the critical zone, the tendency of the rate of profit to fall has to be contained and the pressure on the rate of

---

56. Ankie Hoogvelt, *Globalization and the Postcolonial World*, Palgrave, 2001, p152.

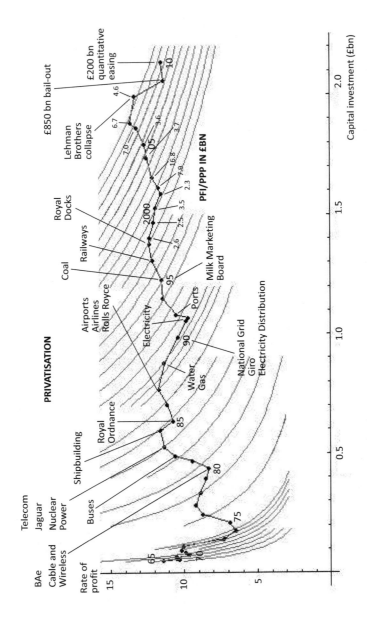

Figure 4.6 UK economic footprint (1965–2010) highlighting the sequence of privatisations and PFI contracts implemented by successive governments to prevent the economy entering the critical zone

profit to fall any further curtailed. It just cannot fall below the threshold, at least not for any length of time, as the destruction of the capitalist system is threatened. It thus hovers along the critical zone level as demonstrated by the economic footprint of the UK economy (Figure 4.5).

In the classical zone, where the rate of profit is high, the pressure on it to fall can be relieved, for a time at least, by allowing it to fall. Here, a falling rate of profit acts like a safety valve which reduces the pressure on the system while allowing profits to rise. In the critical zone, a further fall in the rate of profit is not an option. All the pressure on the rate of profit to fall must be absorbed and counterbalanced by measures that will either directly increase the rate of profit and/or increase profits – measures that have been used with increasing frequency since the 1980s. Their use has been most pronounced since the collapse of Lehman Brothers in 2007.

Measures to lift the rate of profit include freezing or reducing pay levels, increasing pension contributions, worsening terms and conditions, including increased workload and longer working hours, and restricting trade union activities. Measures to increase profits include capital injection (eg contracting out, privatisation, the creation of entry points for private operators into publicly funded enterprises such as the NHS, schools and colleges and council services, as well as PFI), the removal of unproductive capital (eg writing off capital made obsolete as a result of technological advance and the removal of unprofitable capital from production for profit through temporary nationalisation) and increasing turnover.

While the actions listed above may take capital out of the critical zone, the danger of it slipping back remains a haunting possibility. While the characteristic curve may move away from the critical zone the tendency of the rate of profit to fall continues, maintaining the downward pressure as capital continues to accumulate. For this reason, the measures taken to lift the economy out of the critical zone not only have to persist but also have to intensify, with more drastic measures taken year on year. Failure to maintain and intensify these measures may take capital back into the critical zone, with all the dangers that it poses. In this battle, there is no let up and no relief. At this ultimate stage of its development, capitalism is at the edge of a vortex, skating precariously along the edge, and permanently in danger of tipping over.

CHAPTER 5

Saviours of the Environment or Apologists for Capitalism?

Earlier, in Chapter 3, we discussed the economic ideology of the mainstream environmental movement, which comes under the generic heading of 'new economics', with its relaxed approach to scientific analysis in contrast to the thorough and methodical approach of the classicists – Adam Smith, David Ricardo and Karl Marx (who saw political economy as a science). This chapter looks at the ideas and proposals which stem from this underlying ideology, including the no-growth strategy and steady-state economy and such proposals as the polluter pays principle, carbon trading and carbon emission credit. We will start with the anti-growth fetishism.

To grow or not to grow?

The debate about the desirability of growth as an aim for governments is not new. It dates back to the 1970s with such books as Hirsch's *Social Limits to Growth* (1977) and the 1972 *Limits to Growth* report of the Club of Rome. However, the debate gained increased momentum as the ecological crisis took root and became part of everyday discourse. The importance given to growth – what is referred to as the 'obsession with GNP', and what Clive Hamilton calls a fetish – is seen as a stand-alone phenomenon, a matter of individual choice by economists or a collective decision by government and society that can be turned on and off. It must be the first time in economic history that a necessity has been described as a fetish. You might as well describe fish having a fetish for water as capitalism having a fetish for growth. Growth is as essential to capitalism as is water to fish. As fish would die without water, so would capitalism drown without growth.

Gross national product (GNP) is an index of the value of the output of goods and services in a country within a given period, normally a year. Sometimes GDP (gross domestic product),[1] is used, which is a slightly different way of measuring economic output. Both provide a measure of the performance not so much of the economy as of corporations. It is not just the absolute value of GNP or GDP that is

---

1. GNP is defined as the total value of all goods and services produced by firms owned by the country concerned within a given time period, usually a year. GDP includes the production of foreign-owned firms within the country, but excludes the income from domestically owned firms located abroad. Thus, GNP is the gross domestic product plus income earned by domestic residents from foreign investments, minus income earned during the same period by foreign investors in the country's domestic market.

considered to be important, but their rate of change, year on year. The greater the rate, the better the shape of the economy and the country.

The opponents of growth advance two separate and inter-linked objections to growth as a policy objective: on one hand, growth per se, and certainly beyond a certain level, does not bring about greater quality of life (and if anything it is responsible for many of the ills of society);[2] and, on the other hand, even if it did bring happiness, we can't have it because it cannot be sustained indefinitely.

In a new take on an old theme of 'money does not bring you happiness', some environmentalists argue that contentment is not synonymous with increased GNP/GDP. Books have been written and surveys have been conducted to show this: 'The GDP takes only one measure of progress into account: activity; economic activity,' say McDonough and Braungart,[3] while George Monbiot claims that '[t]here is plenty of evidence that as we become richer, we become less content with ourselves'.[4,5] Jonathon Porritt asserts that 'once

---

2. Tim Jackson goes as far as to blame the financial meltdown of 2007–08 on growth: 'And yet allegiance to growth was the single most dominant feature of economic and political systems that led the world to the brink of disaster', *Prosperity Without Growth*, Earthscan, 2011, p21.

3. McDonough and Bruangart, *Cradle to Cradle*, Vintage Digital, 2009, p36.

4. George Monbiot, *Guardian*, 27 August 2002.

5. This evidence is contradicted by other evidence: 'In economics we think that happiness increases with lifetime wealth, albeit at a decreasing rate. But recent research on happiness fails to show a steep gradient between incomes

nations reach a level where most or all of their citizens' basic needs are being met, increases in relative affluence beyond that point does not make much of a difference'.[6] John Foster talks about 'having enough, not having more',[7] and Bookchin rails against 'production for the sake of production'.[8] In *The Loss of Happiness in Market Democracies*, Robert Lane talks about 'the waning power of income to yield that ephemeral good utility'. He continues: 'Academics and politicians receive the greatest blame for being in thrall to the economistic fallacy that, beyond poverty or basic subsistence levels, higher incomes will automatically increase levels of subjective wellbeing.'[9] In support of this theory, reference is often made to a poll which asked 'whether the Government's prime objective should be the "greatest happiness" or the "greatest wealth"': 81% wanted happiness as a goal and only 13% went for wealth.[10] 'The truth of the matter is that economic growth, like the process of

---

and self-reported life satisfaction. But this work has typically focused on rich countries. In a recent paper, Angus Deaton uses Gallup poll data for a large number of countries and uncovers – to my surprise, at least – that people in poor countries are indeed less "happy" on average than people in rich countries', (http://rodrik.typepad.com/dani_rodriks_weblog/2008/02/poor-and-happy.html.

6. Jonathon Porritt, *Capitalism as if the World Matters*, Earthscan, 2007, p61.
7. John Foster, *Ecology Against Capitalism*, Monthly Review Press, 2002, p80.
8. Murray Bookchin, *Towards an Ecological Society*, Black Rose Books, 1995, p67.
9. Robert Lane, *The Loss of Happiness in Market Democracies*, Yale University Press, 2001.
10. Jonathon Porritt, 2007, op cit, p61.

globalisation, has become fixed in people's mind as a given,'[11] says Porritt. 'Far from there being any automatic increase in wellbeing for every increase in levels of consumption, much of our current consumption is turning out to be a very inadequate surrogate for meeting human needs in a more satisfying, durable way.'[12] He cites William Nordhaus and James Tobin, 'two of the world's most eminent economists', who, 35 years ago, criticised the use of GNP as the sole indicator of economic progress:

'...maximising of GNP is not a proper policy objective. Economists all know that, and yet their everyday use of GNP as the standard measure of economic performance conveys the impression that they are evangelistic worshippers of GNP.'[13]

If it is the case that the majority of people prefer 'happiness' to 'wealth' and 'economists all know that' and yet continue in the old way regardless, then surely this is something that ought to be investigated and analysed – yet that is precisely what the anti-growth proponents fail to do. It is like a biologist who, upon encountering scores of salmon fighting their way upstream, declares them suffering from some form of insanity or derangement instead of investigating why they expend such energy and go through unimaginable hardship to get to their destination.

---

11. Ibid, p60.
12. Ibid, p64.
13. Ibid, p10.

In his book *Growth Fetish* (2004), Clive Hamilton blames growth for practically everything that is wrong in the world: skewed priorities of individuals, materialism overtaking society, greediness, sick society, business exercising enormous political power, depression, crime and drug abuse, youth suicide, and poverty – not to mention environmental decline in all its aspects from global warming and climate change to deforestation and pollution. The only thing that growth is not responsible for seems to be earthquakes and tsunamis.

What is being suggested is that this 'obsession with growth' is a psychological obsession, a sort of collective whim that simultaneously grips all governments and all economists worldwide, or some kind of elaborate global conspiracy. Or could the truth be that GNP is not and was never intended to be a measure of the wellbeing of the economy or society, but is rather a measure of the wellbeing of the corporate sector and, as such, any 'obsession with growth' is effectively an obsession with the wellbeing of corporations?

If GNP is not to be used as a policy objective, then what is? Fred Hirsch admits that, while there is reason to be wary of equating GNP with economic performance, there is 'no clear notion of what to put in its place'.[14] Others dust off JS Mill's utilitarianism and Bentham's dictum 'create all the happiness you are able to create, remove all the misery you are able to remove' to bring back to life the notion of 'the greatest

---

14. Fred Hirsch, *Social Limits to Growth*, Routledge, 1977, p55.

happiness' to replace GNP as the aim of economic policy. Clive Hamilton proposes a Genuine Progress Indicator.[15] In his book *Happiness*, Professor Richard Layard defines happiness as 'feeling good',[16] which must rank as the most immeasurable concept invented, though he insists otherwise. He goes on to argue that people 'are happier if they are thankful for what they have'.[17]

All of which is nothing more than the old adage 'better poor and happy, than rich and miserable' – a notion that has long been promulgated by the spokesmen of the wealthy, the landowners and the bourgeoisie and reinforced by the Christian Church and other religions to temper the poor and soothe their anger, to make them feel grateful for what little they have and accept their lot. This moral of many a fairy tale is now turned into an economic policy for an advanced industrial society. And just like a fairy tale, all it takes is a handsome prince or a kind king to spread happiness to everyone and they all live happily ever after. The idea that all it takes to spread happiness is to persuade governments to change their economic priorities was debunked by Bookchin:

'It requires a grotesque self-deception, or worse, an act of ideological social deception, to foster the belief that this society

---

15. Clive Hamilton, *Growth Fetish*, Pluto Press, 2004, p55.
16. 'Happiness is feeling good, and misery is feeling bad', Richard Layard, *Happiness*, Penguin Books, 2006, p6.
17. Ibid, p8.

can undo its very law of life in response to ethical arguments or intellectual persuasion.'[18]

Bookchin's 'law of life' is, of course, the law of the capitalist mode of production, the labour law of value.

The ecological economists, who complain that growth or GNP is only one measure of progress when there are other more important measures, are disingenuous in that they all, to one degree or another, presume that growth will take place (a sort of unspoken precondition). Assume that the government did change its priority from growth to a happiness index (call it the Gross Domestic Happiness Index), something that combines all the elements that make the 'good life'. In pursuance of such a priority, the government collects taxes and makes appropriate resource allocations and welfare provisions. Meanwhile, economic activity goes on in the background. All is well until the economy falters and fails to grow or, even worse, starts to contract as inevitably happens under the capitalist mode of production. For by simply changing government priorities, capitalism is not banished; it continues to work in all its 'glory', including the occasional recession here and there. In such a downturn, as businesses begin to close and people are made redundant, where does the 'happiness' agenda go? How 'happy' is a society with 5, 10 or 15% unemployment?

---

18. Murray Bookchin, *Towards an Ecological Society*, Black Rose Books, 1995, p66.

In the post-2007 financial meltdown, it was the green agenda which came to the rescue of capitalism in its hour of need with suggestions for 'getting the economy going' and growing with such initiatives as the 'Green Economy Initiative to Get the Global Markets Back to Work' launched by UNEP (the United Nations Environment Programme) in October 2008. In *Affluenza* Oliver James cites Denmark as the example of the greatest happiness principle; it 'scores highly in all key indices of wellbeing' he says.[19] This is how Denmark fared in the 2008–09 crisis:

'Since the summer of 2008, the Danish rate of unemployment has increased dramatically. Thus the registered unemployment rate for March 2010 was 4.2 percent, more than a doubling from its lowest level of 1.6 percent in June 2008 (seasonally adjusted). The unemployment rate according to the European Labour Force Surveys (LFS) was 7.6 percent in March 2010 compared to 2.6 percent in June 2008.'[20]

In this case, the only high index seems to be unemployment. Tim Jackson, Professor of Sustainable Development at the University of Surrey and author of *Prosperity Without Growth*, maintains that the solution to the problem of unemployment is sharing the work:

---

19. Oliver James, *Affluenza*, Vermilion, 2007, p102.
20. European Union, EEO Ad Hoc Request, *Long-term Unemployment in Denmark*, May 2010.

'We could also systematically set about sharing out the available work more evenly across the population. Essentially, this means reducing working hours, a shorter working week and increased leisure time... [A]s a route to prevent large-scale unemployment, sharing the available work has much to recommend it.'[21]

The sharing of work would be carried out 'through appropriate working time and employment practices'.[22] But would these employment practices guarantee the same take-home pay or will wages suffer a drop? If it is the former, production costs will increase, resulting in a sharp fall in rates of profit and threatening to bring profits down. Unless firms are able to absorb these losses, they will go bankrupt, leading to further unemployment, more work sharing and further increases in costs. Profits will again fall, with more closures, and so on. When capital is operating in the classical zone, with relatively high rates of profit, such a course of action is possible. By increasing their capital outlay, a corporation's profits can go up even if its rate of profit has suffered a drop. This was the case in the 1960s and early 1970s where claims for 10, 20, 30 and even 45% pay increases were submitted by trade unions, and in the vast majority of cases conceded in full.[23]

---

21. Tim Jackson, *Prosperity Without Growth*, Earthscan, 2011, p134.
22. Ibid, p199.
23. In April 1970 two newspaper publishing trade unions, SOGAT and SLADE, submitted a claim for 25% increased wages. After a 10-day strike, an offer of

This was the situation when capital operated in the classical zone, which Karl Popper thought to be the default situation of capitalism when he wrote that:

'[a successful average capitalist] sees his income rise quickly, and his capital still more quickly; that is to say, his savings rise more quickly than the part of his income which he consumes. I do not think that this is a situation which must force him to desperate measures, or which makes a compromise with the workers impossible. On the contrary, it seems to me quite tolerable.'[24]

Well, it did not seem to be at all tolerable when the economy dived towards the critical zone in 1973–74. Far from making compromises, capitalists chose to lay off workers or went bankrupt rather than concede wage demands. One of the first indications of this approach was in 1971 when 400 toolroom workers at Rolls Royce, Hillingdon, walked out accusing the company of 'lethargy' in dealing with a pay claim of £5. Management refused to continue negotiations while the strike

---

a 5% increase on earnings or 10% on basic pay, whichever was the greater, and an extra week's holiday was conceded. This was not unique. In the same year, workers at GKN-Sankey, Wellington, claimed increases of 45%, dock workers submitted a claim for the basic time rate to be raised from £11 1s. 9d. to £20 (an 80% increase) and at Alcoa Ltd., Waunarlwydd, near Swansea, an increase of 1s. 9d. an hour (about 20%) was agreed following a strike.

24. Karl Popper, *The Open Society*, Volume 2, Routledge, 2003, p202.

continued, and began lay-offs. When 6000 out of a labour force of 8000 had been laid off, the strikers accepted a union call to return to work so that negotiations could resume. A month later, in February 1971, the Rolls Royce bankruptcy was announced.

If job sharing is to lead to a drop in wages, then job sharing is simply unemployment by another name. If 100 unemployed people share the work that 200 fully employed people do, we end up with 300 people each doing two-thirds of a full-time job, or 300 semi-employed people with correspondingly reduced wages. Essentially 200 full-time jobs will be replaced with 300 people working part time.

There is nothing novel about sharing work and increasing leisure time; it is a laudable ambition. Fighting for a shorter working week has been a persistent aim of trade unions for centuries with some notable successes, including the 8-hour day. However, with the economy skirting at the edge of the critical zone, far from reduced working hours, the trend of late has been the reverse: '[A]fter a period of long-term decline the proportion of employees working over 48 hours a week rose through most of the 1990s.'[25] Figures from the Office for National Statistics show that in 2011, full-time employees in the UK worked an average of 42.7 hours a week, compared with 39.3 hours for men and 36.8 hours for women in 1989. The only decrease in working hours has been as a result of part-time employment replacing full-time jobs.

---

25. DTI, Research Series No. 16, 2003.

Part-time working went up from 24% of all employment in 1992 to 27% in 2011[26] with '5.26 million people across the UK clocking up an average seven hours 12 minutes unpaid overtime a week'.[27] As for 'increased leisure time', a 'survey, which polled 3,000 people, said 13% of Londoners spend up to 60 hours a week working – meaning a fifth of those living in the capital have just three hours of "me time" a week'.[28]

THE LIMITS TO GROWTH

The second objection raised against GNP as a policy priority is that it is unsustainable, both in terms of limited natural resources – which makes continued economic growth untenable – and in terms of population growth, outstripping economic growth and increasing poverty. On the resource front, John Foster argues that:

'A 3 percent annual average rate of growth in the world output would mean that world production would double every 23 years; in a single century, it would increase 16 times... It is highly unlikely that the planet could long sustain exponential growth of this kind involving doubling of economic output every quarter century, without experiencing worldwide ecological catastrophe.'[29]

---

26. ONS, December 2011.
27. TUC, 22 February 2011.
28. *Guardian*, 4 January 2010.
29. John Foster, *Ecology Against Capitalism*, Monthly Review Press, 2002, p80.

As for the growth of population, it is seen by some as a pivotal element of the environmental crisis. Paul and Anne Ehrlich put it this way:

'Global warming, acid rain, depletion of the ozone layer, vulnerability to epidemics, and exhaustion of soils and ground-water are all ... related to population size.'[30]

The all-encompassing 'limits to growth' concept was given wide publicity in 1972 when the Club of Rome's *Limits to Growth* (a report described by Barry Commoner as 'widely-publicised but less widely acclaimed for its scientific soundness'[31]) was published. The report concluded that:

'If the present growth trends in world population, industrialization, pollution, food production, and resource depletion continue unchanged, the limits to growth on this planet will be reached some time within the next one hundred years. The most probable result will be a rather sudden and uncontrollable decline in both population and industrial capacity.'

These conclusions are based on the proposition that the Earth has finite resources. Non-renewable resources such as fossil fuel, metals and other minerals are clearly finite. Renewable

---

30. Paul and Anne Ehrlich, *The Population Explosion*, Arrow, 1991, p17.
31. Barry Commoner, *Making Peace with the Planet*, Victor Gollancz, 1990, p104.

resources such as soils, fisheries and forests will replenish themselves; as long as their use does not exceed critical thresholds; however, with current excessive utilisation, they too would become exhausted.

'In pursuit of economic growth, conventional economists almost exclusively put the emphasis on the non-physical parameters of the economy (income choice, distribution, productivity and so on) and expect the physical side to be adjusted accordingly,' says Jonathon Porritt.[32] He cites the second law of thermodynamics as proof of the physical limits to growth. As we have learned previously, the second law of thermodynamics states that in all energy exchanges, in a closed system where no energy enters or leaves the system, the potential energy (the energy stored in natural resources such as fossil fuel, wood, etc) that can be transformed into useful work will always be less at the end of an exchange than at the beginning. It is argued that, with the Earth being such a closed system (like a spaceship isolated in space), if we continue to burn fuel and utilise other forms of potential energy embodied in natural resources to produce commodities and services, the availability of potential energy from these natural resources unremittingly diminishes with time. Conclusion: we are all doomed!

While it is true that the finite amounts of essential resources do set a limit to economic growth, the Earth is not a closed system sustained only by its own limited resources, and thus

---

32. Jonathon Porritt, *Capitalism as if the World Matters*, Earthscan, 2007, p71.

the ultimate limit, as cellular biologist Barry Commoner puts it, is 'the rate at which renewable, solar energy can be recaptured and used'. Indeed, had the Earth been a closed system, there would have been neither plants nor animals nor for that matter fossil fuels, for they all depend on energy from an outside source, namely the Sun. Barry Commoner puts it this way:

'The "limit to growth" approach is based on a serious misconception about the global ecosystem. It depends upon the idea that the Earth is like a spaceship, a closed system isolated from outside sources of support and necessarily sustained only by its own limited resources. But the ecosphere is not in fact a closed, isolated system, for it is totally dependent on the huge influx of energy from an outside source – the sun.'

He goes on: 'In sum, the global ecosystem is not, in the basic thermodynamic sense, an isolated, self-sufficient system.'[33] The contribution made by the Sun is not just essential, it is also substantial: 'Thousands of times the amount of energy needed to fuel human activities hits the surface of the planet every day in the form of sunlight.'[34] It is estimated that 'every square km of desert sands receives the solar equivalent of 1.5 million barrels of oil every year'.[35]

---

33. Barry Commoner, *Making Peace with the Planet*, Victor Gollancz, 1990, pp104–5.
34. McDonough and Bruangart, *Cradle to Cradle*, North Point Press, 2002, p32.
35. Jonathon Porritt, *Capitalism as if the World Matters*, Earthscan, 2007, p189.

What is more pertinent is that the energy transfer from
potential to kinetic energy[36] (in the process of commodity
production) does not take place in isolation – it is conditioned
by the prevailing economic system, the prevailing mode
of production. To grow or not to grow? The impetus
and constraints to growth are as much resource based as
economically determined. The feudal society may have wished
for a high rate of growth, but its relations of production – its
economic system – did not provide for growth. In fact in
the whole of the Middle Ages, which spanned a millennium,
the annual growth rate is estimated to have been between 0
and 0.1%. That wasn't a decision taken by a feudal lord or
the desire of this or that king, but was a consequence of the
prevailing economic conditions.

Equally, today's 'obsession with growth' is not a decision
made by governments or economists based on some
intellectual or ethical premise, but it is an economic imperative
made inevitable by the very dynamics of the capitalist mode
of production. Growth is in its DNA, without which there
can be no capitalism. This is by no means original. It has been
outlined by Karl Marx and since then re-stated by numerous
writers in a variety of ways.[37] Growth is only a 'problem'

---

36. Kinetic energy is energy associated with a particle's movement and as such it
represents all forms of energy such as electric (movement of electrons) and
light (movement of photons).
37. 'It is the single-minded obsession with capital accumulation that
distinguished capitalism from any other social systems, explaining why it can

under the capitalist system of production and exchange. To be tackled, a system other than capitalism, a post-capitalist system, has to evolve, in which case the 'growth problem' would no longer be a problem.

By emphasising the limits to growth and how we must lower the expectations of people in both the developed and developing economies, the anti-growth environmentalists pave the way for lower standards of living, lower pay and worsening conditions – in a word, austerity; precisely what the financiers are demanding in the aftermath of the financial meltdown of 2008.

SOLUTIONS TO THE GROWTH PROBLEM

Proposed solutions to 'problems of growth' are plentiful. There are those who call for a no-growth or 'steady-state' economy, others accept the need for some growth and call for sustainable development or sustainable growth, and there are those who demand population control. Let's examine these proposals in turn.

---

never stand still. Competition of the sort that forces upon capital continual transformation in the means of production in order to maintain and enhance profitability provides the essential motor behind this drive to accumulate... Caught up in this unrelenting process of accumulation, and creative destruction, the system runs roughshod over each and every thing that stands in its path', John Foster, *Ecology Against Capitalism*, Monthly Review Press, 2002, p96.

Sustainable development

Sustainable development was first introduced as a concept in 1987 by *Our Common Future*, also known as the Brundtland Report, which defined it as 'development that meets the needs of the present without compromising the ability of future generations to meet their own needs'. David Pearce, the author of the British government's *Blueprint for a Green Economy*, defines it as 'continuously rising, or at least non-declining, consumption per capita, or GNP, or whatever the agreed indicator of development is'.[38] He divided sustainable development into two main categories: weak and strong. The weak sustainability which provides for 'modified economic growth' guided by economic incentive instruments, eg pollution charges, with the 'caring for others' ethical dimension. Strong sustainability advocates 'zero economic growth and zero population growth', a 'steady-state economy regulated by macro-environmental standards', with interests of the collective overriding those of the individual. Looked at in these terms, sustainable growth falls in to the former category.

Sustainable development is quite different to reducing economic growth argues David Pearce:

> *[It] involves sustaining the overall stock of natural resources so that they are available for the future, as well as for the present... a sustainable future in which both outputs and*

---

38. DW Pearce, *Blueprint 3*, Earthscan, 1996, p8.

inputs are sustained... It broadens the concern with output so that it embraces social goals other than GNP.'[39]

Sustaining the overall stock of natural resources is achieved by ensuring that these resources are part of the market:

'A free market economist would argue that we do not need to encourage sustainability. It will happen naturally... The problem with this solution is that the resources that are most threatened are those without markets: the receiving capacities of the oceans, atmosphere and stratosphere for example, and the greater part of the world's biological diversity. Free markets are not environmentally benign even when they exist. No-one can argue that they can be expected to resolve environmental problems "naturally" if they do not exist at all.'[40]

The instrument through which natural resources are to become part and parcel of the market is based on the concept of 'internalisation'. This maintains that environmental costs are 'unpaid costs' and as such should be included as expenditure by the producer through such schemes as 'polluter pays', carbon trading, and carbon emission credit. As we shall presently see, internalising environmental costs results in the public at large paying for 'sustainability'.

---

39. Ibid, pp4–5.
40. Ibid, p5.

The aim of internalisation is to shift technology in a more energy-efficient direction – towards, for example, improved mileage for cars, replacement of fossil fuels with solar energy and, of course, recycling. But the introduction of more energy-efficient technology does not necessarily mean less pollution if increased efficiency is coupled with increased demand for these natural resources. This has been called the Jevons Paradox, after William Stanley Jevons, best known for his work *The Coal Question* (1865). Jevons 'argued that increased efficiency in using a natural resource, such as coal, only resulted in increased demand for that resource, not a reduction in demand. This was because such improvement in efficiency led to a rising scale of production'.[41] In Jevons' words:

'It is wholly a confusion of ideas to suppose that the economical use of fuel is equivalent to a diminished consumption. The very opposite is the truth. As a rule, new modes of economy will lead to an increase of consumption according to a principle recognised in many parallel instances.'[42]

This is purely a rule of capitalism as Jevons explains in the case of coal:

---

41. John Foster, *Ecology Against Capitalism*, Monthly Review Press, 2002, p94.
42. William Stanley Jevons, *The Coal Question*, Ch 7.

'[It is not] difficult to see how this paradox arises. The number of tons of coal used in any branch of industry is the product of the number of separate works, and the average number of tons consumed in each. Now, if the quantity of coal used in a blast-furnace, for instance, be diminished in comparison with the yield, the profits of the trade will increase, new capital will be attracted, the price of pig-iron will fall, but the demand for it increase; and eventually the greater number of furnaces will more than make up for the diminished consumption of each. And if such is not always the result within a single branch, it must be remembered that the progress of any branch of manufacture excites a new activity in most other branches, and leads indirectly, if not directly, to increased inroads upon our seams of coal.'

This rule continues to apply today. As John Foster observed in the case of cars: 'The introduction of more energy-efficient automobiles in [the US] in the 1970s did not curtail the demand for fuel because driving increased and the number of cars on the road soon doubled.'[43]

Irrespective of the various appeals and incentives to reduce energy consumption, as far as corporations are concerned, increased sales of their products (motor car or energy supply) is a business priority and they will do whatever it takes to promote their product.

---

43. John Foster, *Ecology Against Capitalism*, Monthly Review Press, 2002, p95.

No-growth, post-growth economy

Proponents of no-growth or post-growth economies say that sustainable growth is impossible or, in the words of Herman Daly, that 'the term "sustainable growth" when applied to the economy is bad, an oxymoron – self-contradictory as prose, and unevocative as poetry'.[44] Clive Hamilton, the author of *Growth Fetish*, bases his post-growth society on the assertion that capitalism has solved 'the economic problem'. This is a reference to Keynes' prediction that 'the economic problem, the struggle for subsistence' will be solved and 'man will be faced with his real, his permanent problem, how to use his freedom from pressing economic cares, how to occupy the leisure':

> *'I draw the conclusion that, assuming no important wars and no important increase in population, the economic problem may be solved, or be at least within sight of solution, within a hundred years. This means that the economic problem is not – if we look into the future – the permanent problem of the human race.'*[45]

Thus Hamilton speaks of the problem of scarcity having been solved with his 'post-scarcity' society and his conviction that

---

44. Herman Daly and Kenneth Townsend, *Valuing the Earth*, MIT Press, 1996, p267.
45. John Maynard Keynes, *Essays in Persuasion*, section on Economic Possibilities for our Grandchildren, WW Norton & Co, 1963, pp358–73.

we now live in 'the age of abundance': 'It must be accepted that capitalism has moved to a phase of abundance, and abundance broadly spread.'[46] As proof of such abundance, Hamilton writes:

> *'With more wealth at their disposal than ever before, most people could simply not participate – to step off the materialist treadmill, to ignore the advertisements, to eschew the latest electronic gadgets, the second house, the luxury car, the holidays abroad, the meaningless acquisitions.'*[47]

Hamilton obviously lives in a different world than most of humanity. The world for many of us is one of hard work and making ends meet; not so much of holidays abroad as holidays if at all possible. Not so much second homes as homes repossessed. Not so much not wanting to participate as unable to. The 'post-scarcity society' and the 'age of abundance' is a society of abundance for the few and scarcity for the many.

Clive Hamilton contends that 'the arrival of the age of abundance for the first time provides the possibility of the liberation of work'. He hastens to add that by 'liberation of work it should not be taken to mean liberation from work':

> *'Because of technological and organisational advance we are vastly wealthier, so that survival through working long hours is no longer the only option. A large proportion of the*

---

46. Clive Hamilton, *Growth Fetish*, Pluto Press, 2004, pxv.
47. Ibid.

labour force can choose to work more or less. Only about half of the workforce is now non-managerial employees of private firms. The rest are managers, self employed, or employees of the public sector... So, for a significant proportion of the workforce in Western society, the chains of wage labour have fallen away.' [48]

Hamilton's 'liberation of work' is not dissimilar to a starving man's liberation of food. According to Hamilton: 'In countries where the "economic problem" has been solved it is no longer necessary or desirable to think of work primarily as a means of material survival.'[49] The assumption here is that in the age of abundance work is no longer paramount, which begs the question: who exactly is producing so much abundance that people can choose to 'work more or less'? The paradox of Hamilton's argument is that, while he calls for no growth, he bases his whole post-growth, post-scarcity society on a level of abundance, which he later promotes to a 'superabundance'[50] that can only have been brought about by super growth.

According to Hamilton, employees of the public sector can choose to 'work more or less' and the self-employed just swan around and work as they feel like it. As for managers, well they don't work at all which begs the question: why are they the group most likely to suffer from work-related stress? It is

48. Ibid.
49. Ibid, p147.
50. Ibid, p163.

certainly not because of having too much leisure time on their hands. Hamilton himself quotes William Bridges writing in *Fortune* magazine:

> *'We used to read predictions that by the year 2000 everyone would be working 30-hour weeks and the rest would be leisure. But as we approach 2000, it seems more likely that half of us would be working 60-hour weeks and the rest of us would be unemployed. What's wrong?'*[51]

Irrespective of all the evidence, Hamilton insists 'the superabundance of modern capitalism has liberated people from the need to cling to a career path', or the need for security of employment, and that 'the shift to self-employment and the spread of part-time work are laying the foundation for a post-growth society',[52] which, far from ushering in a post-growth future, will be precisely the changes that will bring about the flexibility that capitalism strives for – and with it higher growth.

Steady-state economy

The first recorded attempt at a steady state was King Canute's. His idea of a steady-state sea level, in which the flow and ebb of the tide would be banished, has great advantages, not least that sailing boats would be able to set out to sea at any time of

---

51. Ibid, p158.
52. Ibid, pp170–71.

day or night. However, there was one tiny flaw in his logic: the gravitational force of the moon which creates the movement of the tide. The advocates of the steady-state capitalist economy are on the same shore as King Canute.

The steady-state economy advocated by Herman Daly among others expands the theme of 'no growth' to include population. The steady-state economy is John Stuart Mill's stationary state regurgitated, which he defined as a 'stationary condition of capital and population'. In a manner familiar to those with religious beliefs, Mill asks: '... to what goal? Towards what ultimate point is society tending by its industrial progress?' The 'stationary state' is the ultimate aim: '... at the end of what [political economists] call the progressive state lies the stationary state, that all progress in wealth is but a postponement of this, and that each step in advance is an approach to it.'[53]

The concept of a steady state or stationary state is familiar to engineers and scientists when analysing the operation of a system such as an internal combustion engine or an electronic control system. A system in a steady state is one whose output either does not fluctuate or, if it does, it is quickly brought back to a steady state by feedback loops which carry out such corrections and controls as necessary to bring the output back to a steady-state level within a reasonable time span.

For instance, an electric iron has a steady state which keeps the temperature of the ironing surface steady as the iron is

---

53. JS Mill, *Principles of Political Economy*, 1848, Book 4, Ch 6.

used and heat is transferred from the iron to the material being ironed. In this case, a thermostat switch is used which senses the temperature of the iron surface and consequently closes to feed mains power to the heating element or opens to stop electric power going to the heating element as its temperature changes. However, this very same system would not have a steady state if, for instance, the power from the mains supply was erratic, changing its voltage level beyond specified limits and/or turning on and off at will. Similarly, if the material being ironed is at a very low temperature, say near freezing, then the iron may not be able to settle at its steady-state temperature.

The same applies to other systems, such as a radio receiver which has automatic gain control (a.g.c). The purpose of a.g.c. is to control the gain of the radio frequency amplifier to ensure that the sound level remains constant as the received signal changes in strength due to such things as changing atmospheric conditions or movement, as in the case of a car radio. In general, a.g.c. works well, but the reader may have had instances of a sound breakdown, albeit momentarily. This is because the radio signal is so low that it could not be counterbalanced by the a.g.c. loop.

In general, therefore, a steady state is conditioned by the state of both the input and the output of the system, as well as its internal design. It follows, therefore, that, before one can talk about a steady state of the economy, one must ask if the operation of the economic system – its inner workings, its laws and inter-relations – allow for a steady state. We will see presently that growth is as necessary to the capitalist mode of production as water is to fish. But for the time being let us look further at the no-growth and the steady-state propositions and ask if growth can be an optional extra.

Growth – optional extra or intractable necessity?

Herman Daly and Clive Hamilton do not ask whether growth, as far as capitalism is concerned, is an optional extra that can be tamed or discarded at will, or whether it is an intrinsic part of the system. Herman Daly pays homage to JS Mill and considers his discussion of the stationary state 'even more relevant today than in his own time',[54] while Clive Hamilton notes that 'Mill declared that he had no aversion to a stationary state of capital and wealth',[55] as if capitalism needed Mill's permission before proceeding along the no-growth road.[56] Tim Jackson, however, confronts the question directly and asserts that the presumption that growth is a necessary condition for a capitalist economy is 'false in general'.[57]

---

54. Herman Daly and Kenneth Townsend, *Valuing the Earth*, MIT Press, 1996, p28.
55. Clive Hamilton, *Growth Fetish*, Pluto Press, 2004, p9.
56. This is what JS Mill wrote: 'I cannot, therefore, regard the stationary state of capital and wealth with the unaffected aversion so generally manifested towards it by political economists of the old school. I am inclined to believe that it would be, on the whole, a very considerable improvement on our present condition', JS Mill, *Principles of Political Economy*, Book 4, Ch 6, para 5.
57. Tim Jackson, *Prosperity Without Growth*, Earthscan, 2011, p198.

Growth, or capital accumulation, plays a central role in the health of the capitalist economy so much so that even small changes in capital accumulation can bring about a severe economic crisis. This is how Keynes explained it: During a boom, profits are made, capital accumulates and investment is increased in anticipation of future demand. 'It is natural and reasonable', he wrote, 'that expectations of the future should play a dominant part in determining the scale on which new investment is deemed advisable. But ... the basis of such increased investment is very precarious. Being based on shifting and unreliable evidence, they are subject to sudden and violent changes.' Increased investment is coupled with reduced 'marginal efficiency' of capital:

'But the essence of [a slump] is to be found, nevertheless, in the collapse in the marginal efficiency of capital, particularly in the case of those types of capital which have been contributing most to the previous phase of heavy investment.'[58]

In other words, the high growth during the boom years resulted in high capital accumulation – so high that there is too much capital that has nowhere to be invested with the expectation of making a profit:

---

58. JM Keynes, *General Theory*, Harcourt Brace Jovanovich, 1964, pp315–8.

'Thus at the outset of the slump there is probably much capital of which the marginal efficiency has become negligible or even negative.'[59]

The very source of a boom – a glut of capital with zero or even negative marginal efficiency – is the cause of the slump. Although Keynes was hailed as a genius in 1935 when the General Theory was published, his analysis was by no means original. Karl Marx, decades before, wrote of 'overproduction of capital' resulting in a fall in the rate of profit and subsequently an economic slump:

'There would be an absolute overproduction of capital as soon as the additional capital for purposes of capitalist production would be equal to zero. As soon as capital would have grown to such a proportion compared with the labouring population, that neither the absolute labour time nor the relative surplus-labour time could be extended any further; as soon as a point is reached where the increased capital produces no larger, or even smaller, quantities of surplus-value than it did before its increase, there would be an absolute overproduction of capital. That is to say, the increased capital C + ΔC would not produce any more profit, or even less profit, than capital C before its expansion by ΔC. In both cases there would be a strong and sudden fall in the average rate of profit.'[60]

---

59. Ibid, p317.
60. Karl Marx, *Capital*, Volume 3, Part 3, Ch 15, para 30.

The process described by Keynes, and Marx before him, is simple: investment is directed towards making a profit, and once profit is made, it is reinvested to make more profit. If there is to be no growth, total capital outlay remains the same with no additional capital investment. Apart from maintenance and/or replacement of depreciated capital (machinery, offices, cars, etc) the capitalist has no means of deploying his or her profit; it remains idle with a marginal efficiency of zero, and it continues to grow, year on year. There would thus be a glut of capital without a home.

As we have seen above, this is the same phenomenon which Keynes said caused the Great Depression, except this time the glut will be increased year on year.[61] The problem won't be solved by spending the profits on goods and services, for demand for these products will increase and, given a no-growth economy, there is no way of satisfying that demand by increasing the supply; prices of these products will increase, which creates even more profits for those enterprises that produce these products – profits that cannot be reinvested, and so on. If the government takes the surplus, the same problem arises; what is the government going to do with it? Waste it (spending it on armament and wars), throw it away? Or spend

---

61. Theoretically speaking, the problem could be solved if every caplitalist decides not to save anything for future use, spends all their profits on goods and services, and these goods and services consumed year on year. This is as likely to happen as a hundred coins rolling down a slope remaining upright without a single coin flipping over even when they reach the end of the slope.

it on welfare? We are back to square one; increased demand for products and services with restricted supply.

Only if profit making is done away with altogether would a no-growth or a steady state be achieved, and that's not on the cards: 'Ecological economists do not call for an end to markets. Markets are necessary,'[62] wrote Herman Daly in *Ecological Economics*: 'Post-growth political philosophy does not represent any fundamental threat to private property,' says Clive Hamilton in the *Growth Fetish*.[63] It follows, therefore, that growth – capital accumulation – far from being one option among many, is a necessary precondition for a mode of production whose sole purpose is the creation of profit.

Advocates of no growth provide brave visions of prosperous economies without growth. But are these proposed economies based on capitalist relations of production or not? For if they are, then you might as well talk of a no-water fish as a no-growth capitalist economy. Tim Jackson argues for a 'less capitalistic' economy[64] in which a 'new investment ecology is likely to change the balance between private and public ownership', where 'the whole economy is underpinned by the revenue generation potential of ecological services. Public sector investment in these assets should, as a matter of principle, seek returns from their productive capabilities.' The economy Tim Jackson envisages has a mixture of private and

---

62. Herman Daly, *Ecological Economics*, Island Press, 2011, p6.
63. Clive Hamilton, *Growth Fetish*, Pluto Press, 2004, p212.
64. Tim Jackson, *Prosperity Without Growth*, Earthscan, 2011, pp200–1.

public ownership; the private would no doubt seek return on their investment and, as for the public sector, it too 'should, as a matter of principle, seek returns from their productive capabilities'. So, it is profit making all round.

THE 'POLLUTER PAYS' PRINCIPLE

Ecological economists argue that capitalism does not take into account the full cost of natural resources and the damage to the environment caused by business. 'Capitalism must be regarded as an economy of unpaid costs,'[65] argues K William Kapp among others. They call for a 'polluter pays' tax to cover the real cost of energy and to compensate for the damage done to the environment so that the 'price for products and services is one that reflects the wider social costs of production inclusive of any environmental services'.[66]

On the surface of it the 'polluter pays' principle sounds reasonable. If corporations had to pay for their pollution, they would be more careful in their use of polluting energy sources and it would be worth their while to devise new techniques to reduce the amount of pollution they produce. But on whose shoulders does the pollution tax fall? David Pearce, et al, argue that although the business pays the tax, 'the polluters can pass

---

65. K William Kapp, *The Social Costs of Private Enterprise*, New York, Schocken Books, 1971, p231.
66. DW Pearce, et al, *Blueprint for a Green Economy*, Earthscan, 1992, p156.

on an increase in the cost of production to consumers... In practice they can pass on only part of the increased cost they bear'.[67] They support their argument by a supply and demand diagram which shows how, by shifting the supply curve by the amount of the tax, price increases and demand decreases, with polluter and customer sharing the increase in price proportionately (depending on the elasticity of the two curves). This is true only if the tax affected one or a restricted number of products and only in the short term. In the medium or long term, given everything else remaining unchanged, the full weight of the tax will be borne by the consumers. However, if the tax was to affect all products and services, all other things being equal, the average rate of profit will fall.

Given the same state of technology, a pollution tax increases the cost of production, which, if not passed to the consumer in the form of an increase in price, would reduce the rate of profit. In the case where the pollution tax is applied to one (or a restricted number) of products or services, the fall in profit in the short term would be shared out between the producer and the customer as outlined by David Pearce, et al. However, in the medium and long term, capital would not be invested in these particular products if the rate of profit is below the prevailing average. This will result in a redistribution of capital investment to equalise the rate of profit. If the product or products affected are a very small proportion of the totality of the national product, the effect on the average rate of profit

67. Ibid, p158.

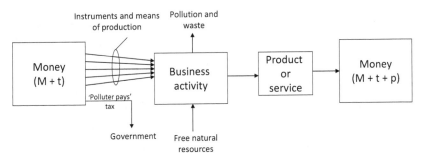

Figure 5.1 Closed system incorporating pollution tax

will be imperceptible and the producers affected by the tax will be able to increase price to offset the tax completely.

Let us redraw the diagram in Figure 3.2 in Chapter 3 to include the pollution tax. This is shown as a cost to the capitalist with the tax going to the government.

With the 'polluter pays' principle, the money advanced has to increase to include the tax that has to be paid by the business, namely M + t where M is the money that would have been paid out before the imposition of the 'polluter pays' tax and t is the tax itself. The capital that has to be advanced for the same level of business activity is now increased to M + t. Once the product or service has been sold, the capitalist would have his or her original capital (M + t) returned together with a profit (p) as shown. If the amount of profit remains the same as before the 'polluter pays' tax was levied, the capitalist suffers from the fact that he had to lay out a larger amount of capital (M + t) for the same amount of profit (p), a reduction in the rate of profit from p/M to p/(M + t), which compared with other possible investment becomes unattractive. In which case the capitalist may either take his capital elsewhere or increase the price of the product or service.

If the capitalist increases the price in order to maintain his rate of profit, two things happen: in the first place, the consumer will pay the pollution tax and not the capitalist, and secondly the capitalist will end up with increased profit. Assuming that a capital outlay of M = £100,000 is invested in an enterprise which produces 10,000 items of a particular product that sells at £11 per item. This will give the capitalist a total income of £11 × 10,000 = £110,000, yielding a profit of £10,000 at the prevailing rate of profit of (10,000/100,000 =) 10%.

Let us now consider the effect of a pollution tax. In order to investigate the effect of the pollution tax in isolation from other changes, we have to assume that all other things remain unchanged, in particular the prevailing rate of profit, and that only technological change that is related to pollution reduction is employed. If, for example, a tax (t) of £5000 is imposed, the total capital outlay would now increase to £100,000 + £5000 = £105,000. Given a prevailing rate of profit of 10%, the profit pocketed by the capitalist would rise to £105,000 × 10% = £10,500, an increase of £500 or 5%. This can only come about if the price of the product goes up from £11 to £11.55 per item (£105,000 + 10,500)/10,000). Each customer now pays 50p per item towards the pollution tax and 5p towards maintaining the capitalist's rate of profit.

The above assumes that all the 10,000 items were sold and there was no effect on demand by the price increase. However, it is possible, depending on the elasticity of the demand, that by increasing the price of the product, sales would suffer a decline. If such a loss occurs, then either the price has to go up even further to compensate for the loss in revenue or the business is scaled down or a combination of both. A price increase may generate a further drop in demand and so on until the market settles at a price at which supply and demand are in equilibrium. The second option, in which the investor takes his capital away, does not affect the above calculations: either the particular product will no longer be produced, or another capitalist comes in who will only invest money if he or she is certain to obtain the prevailing rate of profit – a scenario that takes us back to the previous option. Either way, the price of the product would be higher than before the 'polluter pays' tax was introduced.

In the case where the pollution tax affects all products and services, such as an energy tax, then, other things being equal (the state of technology being one), the rate of profit of all products and services will fall, bringing down the average rate of profit with the cost of the tax shared out between the producer and the customer. This, of course, explains why corporations are so opposed to such taxes without subsidies.

The main argument in favour of the 'polluter pays' tax is that it would encourage corporations to invest in energy-saving techniques in order to avoid paying the tax. This may well be true, but it does not change the above analysis. The cost of the tax would now be replaced by the extra cost of the new energy-saving, low-emission techniques. Only if the cost of these new techniques is considerably lower than the tax would the price of the product drop, but never below the pre-pollution tax level.

ENVIRONMENTALISTS FOR CAPITALISM

Presumably, Jonathon Porritt, having the above in mind and the recognition that 'the very purpose of wealth creation in capitalist economies is to generate profits',[68] was clear in his intention when he invented the concept of 'sustainable profitability', which seeks to accommodate both profit making and sustainability, with companies 'excelling in the pursuit of legitimate profitability while simultaneously making continuous progress towards genuine sustainability.'[69] Precisely what is 'legitimate profitability' and when profit becomes illegitimate are not clear. The impression given is that 'legitimate profitability' may be something less than maximum profitability, so companies whose sole purpose is to maximise profits are to sacrifice some of their profits for the good of the environment. They are not to pass on the cost of sustainability to the customers. Capital will then be 'allocated against a different set of criteria'.

But this goes against the very essence of capitalism (the market and the allocation of resources) and sits very uncomfortably with the author's complete commitment to capitalism and the market: 'The truth of it is that

---

68. Jonathon Porritt, *Capitalism as if the World Matters*, Earthscan, 2007, p92.
69. Ibid.

capitalism, in one form or another, is likely to provide the all-encompassing ideological framework for the foreseeable future.'[70] Recognising the futility of asking corporations to be environmentally conscientious and abandon the pursuit of maximum profit for altruistic reasons, Jonathon Porritt and others urge corporations to consider 'the business case for sustainable development', and that 'the interests of shareholders, over time, are best served by companies that seek radically to improve their social, environmental and ethical performance'.[71] Herman Daly and John Cobb (1989) in *For the Common Good* wrote 'that wealth creation should be organised as to simultaneously optimise both profits and social wellbeing thus making wellbeing and profit morally and ethically equal',[72] thus placing an employer's right to a profit on the same moral and ethical levels as the wellbeing of infants and the disabled.

Stuart Hart has a more direct approach:

'Sustainable global enterprise thus represents the potential for a new private-sector-based approach to development that creates profitable businesses and simultaneously raises the quality of life for the world's poor, respects cultural diversity, and conserves the ecological integrity of the planet for future generations.'[73]

---

70. Ibid, p107.
71. Ibid, p202.
72. Quoted by Porritt, ibid, p279.
73. Stuart Hart, *Capitalism at the Crossroads*, Wharton School Publishing, 2007, pxl.

Let us see how this is supposed to work – how it is possible for corporations to take the environment seriously. Take, for instance, a corporation with a capital outlay of £100 million. At a prevailing rate of profit of say 10%, an investment of £100 million will yield a profit of £10 million. Being public spirited, environmentally conscious and convinced by the argument put forward by Daly, Porritt, Cobb and others, the Chief Executive decides to invest an extra £5 million in equipment that reduces the corporation's carbon emission without passing on the cost to the consumer. While the profit level remains constant at £10 million, the rate of profit of the corporation will change from 10% to (£10/£105 =) 9.52%, a drop of 4.8%. A fall in the rate of profit causes the returns on investment to drop which leads to the corporation's share value falling in the stock exchange, and the Chief Executive will suddenly find it harder to get credit from the banks and, if no action is taken, share values will fall further until the corporation goes bust.

UK supermarket chain Iceland is a good case in point. In June 2000, Malcolm Walker, co-founder and Executive Chairman of Iceland, described by the *Independent* newspaper as one of 'Britain's most prominent and evangelical "green" businessmen who has repeatedly been feted by environmental groups'[74] decided to switch the supermarket chain's entire own-brand frozen vegetable range to organic – at no extra cost to the consumer. The initiative, which removes at a stroke the

---

74. *Independent*, 23 January 2001.

principal consumer objection to organic food – that it costs a lot more – was hailed by such people as Patrick Holden, Director of the Soil Association, and Sandra Bell, real food campaigner at Friends of the Earth, as a promising example of an enlightened corporation that should be followed by others. The supermarket chain also gave the National Trust £1 million to help pay for new green measures on its 700 farms, including converting more to organic status. This was an example of an environmentally conscious major corporation with an enlightened chairman doing the right thing. The experiment lasted a mere six months. In January 2001, the plan was abandoned and the Executive Chairman was replaced. While it began as an example of enlightened corporate action, the case of Iceland ended as an example of the laws of capitalism asserting themselves.

It isn't that the ideas and schemes put forward by the environmentalist movement are without merit; it is just that they rely on the wrong delivery system. Capitalism is the wrong vehicle to deliver sustainable development, combat global warming, allocate resources, utilise carbon capture, reform agriculture or introduce geo-engineering. It is like sending an exploratory satellite station to Mars on a clapped-out rocket that finds it difficult to escape the Earth's gravity, let alone reach the heavens.

Chapter 6

A Crisis Too Far

'There is the potential for not just one crisis but three: a situation where the ATM freezes up, the planet warms up and the light goes out,' wrote Larry Elliott in the *Guardian* recently.[1] And their convergence at this particular time is not a coincidence. The metamorphosis of the financial crisis into an economic recession leads inexorably to increased neglect of the environment as attempts are made to re-ignite the economy at any cost, including devastating cost to the environment.

Four years after the collapse of Lehman Brothers, hopes that what started at Kyoto would flourish into a new climate agreement to take effect before 2016 were dashed. 'The UK, European Union, Japan, US, and other rich nations are all now united in opting to put off any agreement' until well after 2012, the year when the provisions of the Kyoto Protocol, the only legally binding international agreement to limit emissions,

---

1. *Guardian*, 31 May 2011.

expires. This is a prospect which Faith Birol, Chief Economist at the International Energy Agency (and one of the foremost authorities on climate economics), said would forever close the door to keeping the rise of temperatures below 2°C.[2]

Before the 2008 meltdown, it was widely asserted that capitalism was to save the planet through a green revolution. Now, however, it is the green revolution that is being expected to save capitalism; from 'go green to save the planet' to 'go green to save capitalism'. This is best illustrated by the launch of the United Nation's Environment Programme's (UNEP's) Green Economy Initiative which the *Guardian* said 'could revive the stumbling global economy, combat climate change and cut poverty'.[3] In a press release headed 'UNEP Launches Green Economy Initiative to Get the Global Markets Back to Work', UNEP talks about 'seizing an historic opportunity to bring about tomorrow's economy today'. But, can crisis-ridden capitalism be cajoled into action to save the planet or are we witnessing a crisis too far?

In a previous chapter we have seen how capitalism has two phases or zones: the traditional (or conventional) phase and the critical phase. In the conventional phase, rates of profits are high but falling and capital is in relative abundance. In this phase, the fall in the rate of profit is easily compensated for by an increase in investment which itself puts pressure on the rate of profit to fall further and so on until a critical threshold is

---

2. *Guardian*, 21 November 2011.
3. *Guardian*, 23 October 2008, and UNEP press release, 22 October 2008.

reached. In the critical phase the rate of profit is at the critical threshold which, if crossed, would require prohibitively large additional capital investment if profits are to be maintained, let alone improved.

In contrast to the former relative abundance of capital, the critical zone manifests a general deficiency of capital. To prevent capitalism from diving into the critical zone, a huge injection of capital is necessary, as was the case in 1974–75 when the UK characteristic curve – capital's footprint (see Chapter 4) – crossed the critical threshold, ushering in a new kind of crisis. The injection of capital took the form of the sweeping privatisation of the 1980s, the PFI schemes of the 1990s, multi-billion bail-outs and quantitative easing following the financial crisis of 2007. These measures transferred public money into the profit-making sector to the tune of £110 billion in the UK alone. Other countries took similar measures.[4]

While these measures ensured one of the longest periods of economic boom in the UK and other economies,[5] it could not

---

4. 'Privatisation has been imposed by multilateral agencies... By 1992, more than eighty countries around the world had privatised some 6800 previously state-owned enterprises, mainly monopoly suppliers of essential public services such as water, electricity and telecommunications... In total the value of global privatisations in the developing and former socialist world amounted to over US$58bn between 1988 and 1995', Ankie Hoogvelt, *Globalization and the Postcolonial World*, Palgrave, 2001, p153.

5. The euphoria was so high that Chancellor of the Exchequer Gordon Brown proudly announced the end of boom and bust to Parliament on several occasions between 2000 and 2007.

satisfy the ever-increasing demand for capital that the economy needed as it fluctuated along the edge of the critical zone. The inevitable crash came in 2008 – first with a financial meltdown and then with a fully-blown economic recession, comparable only with the Great Depression of the 1930s. But it is not the '30s all over again.

IT IS NOT THE '30S – IT IS FAR WORSE

While the outward symptoms of the Great Crash and the 2008 meltdown are similar – bank failures, economic downturn, unemployment, hardship and near-collapse of the system – the underlying terrains are anything but. In fact they are polar opposites. The 1930s' depression was one of abundance, abundance of capital; that of 2008 is one of deficiency, capital deficiency.

Galbraith in his celebrated book *The Great Crash* wrote: 'The causes of the Depression are still far from certain.'[6] That may or may not be true, but its terrain is well known. It is what Keynes and others refer to as 'over-investment', or under-consumption, and what Marx, a century earlier, called 'over-production';[7] a condition which Keynes described as 'a shortage

---

6. JK Galbraith, *The Great Crash*, Pelican, 1987, p189.
7. 'In these crises, there breaks out an epidemic that, in all earlier epochs, would have seemed an absurdity – the epidemic of over-production. Society suddenly finds itself put back into a state of momentary barbarism; it appears as if a famine, a universal war of devastation, had cut off the supply of every

of houses, but where nonetheless no one can afford to live in the houses that there are'.[8] Keynes agrees with others that over-investment is a normal characteristic of a boom. His analysis differs from the balance-the-budget-at-any-cost advocates in that 'the remedy would not lie in clipping a high rate of interest' but in 'taking drastic steps, by redistributing incomes or otherwise, to stimulate the propensity to consume'.[9]

Galbraith, however, prefers to talk of 'insufficient investment' in the sense of investment that fell short of the available capital at the time. He argues that with output per worker in manufacturing industries increasing by about 43% between 1919 and 1929, and with costs falling and prices not changing, profits increased in the period leading to the 1929 crash. These profits 'encouraged a very high level of capital investment'. He goes on:

'A large and increasing investment in capital goods was, in other words, a principal device by which profits were being spent. It follows that anything that interrupted the investment outlays – anything indeed – which kept them from showing the necessary rate of increase, could cause trouble. When this

---

means of subsistence; industry and commerce seem to be destroyed. And why? Because there is too much civilization, too much means of subsistence, too much industry, too much commerce', Marx and Engels, *Manifesto of the Communist Party.*

8. John Maynard Keynes, *General Theory*, Harcourt Brace Jovanovich, 1964, p322.

9. Ibid, p321.

occurred, compensation through an increase in consumer spending could not automatically be expected. The effect, therefore, of insufficient investment – investment that failed to keep pace with the steady increase in profits – could be falling total demand reflected in turn in falling orders and output.'[10]

According to Galbraith, therefore, investment could not keep up with profits. In short, at the crash of 1929 that led to the Great Depression, there was an excess, an abundance, of capital – capital that could not be profitably invested.[11]

Keynes made a similar analysis, but he preferred to call it over-investment in the sense that too much has been invested, producing goods that could not be sold, which then leads neatly to his remedy of increasing demand to satisfy the supply created by over-investment, as opposed to those who propose the opposite, namely reducing the 'over-investment' so that production is merely enough to satisfy the existing demand. Had the situation not been one of an abundance of capital, Keynes demand-side recipes would not work, for no matter how high a demand is, a bank cannot lend if it does not have the capital to do so. Whichever way it is looked at, the assumption is one of an abundance of capital. This is how Marx described a crisis in general terms:

---

10. JK Galbraith, *The Great Crash*, Pelican, 1987, p193.

11. 'According to a survey of 3,438 manufacturers… 86.4 per cent either did not need to borrow or had no problem doing so', Richard C Koo, *The Holy Grail of Macroeconomics*, Wiley, 2009, p99.

'Nothing is more erroneous, therefore, than to blame a scarcity of productive capital for such a condition. It is precisely at such times that there is a superabundance of productive capital, partly in relation to the normal, but temporarily reduced scale of production, and partly in relation to the paralysed consumption'.[12]

However, when capital enters the critical zone, the capital abundance that characterised previous economic crises turns into deficiency. A new phenomenon is suddenly observed culminating in a crisis of a different type where 'established economic laws' are no longer applicable: 'We are in a completely different world. It is no ordinary recession,' Richard Koo, of the Nomura Research Institute and author of *The Holy Grail of Macroeconomics*, told BBC *Newsnight*. 'This is not what we learned in universities.'[13] In this, he echoed Nobel Prize winner, Joseph Stiglitz who, as we shall see presently, also found that well-established theories predicted outcomes that were vastly different from what actually occurred.

Richard Koo argues that there are two types of recession: 'those that are a natural result of business cycles and those that are attributed to corporate balance sheet'. The 2009 credit crash and subsequent recession, and the recession in Japan which began in the 1990s, are examples of the second kind, what he calls 'balance sheet recession':

---

12. Karl Marx, *Capital*, Volume 3, Ch 30, para 19.
13. *Newsnight*, BBC, 13 December 2011.

*'The balance sheet recession concept … starts with the notion
that certain external shocks actually change the priorities
of firms and households. In particular, a nationwide fall
in asset prices forces firms to shift their priorities from
profit maximisation to repair their balance sheets…*[14]
*[in a situation where] the first priority is no longer profit
maximisation, but debt minimisation.'*[15]

But the fact that one firm may decide to use some or all of its
profit to pay back a bank loan does not make its profit any
smaller; it just means that there will be less money left over
for dividends. If a corporation decides to pay back debts, that
does not mean that it has abandoned profit maximisation.
In fact, only through making a profit can a corporation pay
back debts; and paying back debts itself can, in some cases, be
a means to profit maximisation. It is true that, if a company
spends its cash on paying debts instead of ploughing the
money back into the business, there will probably be less profit
at the end of the year. But that does not necessarily mean that
it is not maximising its profit. Profit maximisation is not the
same as increasing profits. A maximum profit in one year may
be smaller or greater than that of the preceding year, but it
remains the maximum possible for that particular year. Richard
Koo goes on:

---

14. Richard C Koo, *The Holy Grail of Macroeconomics*, Wiley, 2009, p85.
15. Ibid, p15.

'Whether Japanese, American, German or Taiwanese, the
manager of a firm with a healthy business and a positive cash
flow, but deeply troubled balance sheet [caused by a plunge
in domestic asset prices] would respond in the same way:
he or she would use cash flow to pay down debt as quickly
as possible [even if the interest rate is at or near zero]…
When a nationwide plunge in asset prices eviscerates asset
values, leaving only debt behind, the private sector begins
paying down debt en masse. As a result, the broader economy
experiences something economists call "fallacy of composition".
[It] should not be surprising [therefore] that companies
suffering from a debt overhang will not ask to borrow more
just because loans have grown cheaper… During this process
[of repairing the balance sheet] firms put on a bright face for
outside journalists and analysts, discussing their rosy earning
prospects in the hope of diverting attention away from
the balance sheet … [because] the discovery of a balance-
sheet problem by people outside the company would almost
certainly have serious consequences for their credit ratings.' [16]

But surely the knowledge that a corporation's profit is below
that which is possible (or that it has actually made a loss)
will have the very same effect as an unfavourable or negative
balance sheet. With profits below maximum, how is a
corporation to prove its 'rosy earning prospects'? Profits are the
first port of call for any analyst and that's why 'covering up for

---

16. Ibid, pp15–8.

investments that went sour after the 1980s "bubble" economy burst was so widespread in Japan that a special term describes the practice, "tobashi'".[17] In one case in 2011, Olympus had its headquarters raided by the Japanese authorities, who were investigating allegations of deception dating back to the 1990s. It is clear that repairing a balance sheet at the expense of returns on dividends can land a corporation in as much trouble as maximising profit with little regard to the balance sheet.

As for 'fallacy of composition', it is a concept frequently used by economists to shift the focus away from the workings of the economic system to the actions of individuals. Fallacy of composition 'occurs when behaviour that would be right for one person (or company) leads to an undesirable outcome when engaged in by all people (or companies)'.[18] Imagine that there was a fire in a theatre with two exits, one of which was in the vicinity of the fire. Naturally, everyone made for the exit away from the fire, causing a stampede resulting in the death of three people. According to the theory of 'fallacy of composition', heading for the exit away from the fire was the right thing to do on an individual level, but when everyone engaged in the same behaviour, people died. The emphasis is immediately shifted from the cause of the fire to the actions of individuals.

The solution to the 'fallacy of composition' offered by Richard Koo and others is for governments 'to take the

---

17. *Guardian*, 21 December 2011.
18. Richard C Koo, *The Holy Grail of Macroeconomics*, Wiley, 2009, pp15–6.

opposite course of action', thus completely avoiding any examination of what brought about the private sector's reluctance to borrow and invest in the first place. As Richard Koo says, referring to Japan's 1990s recession:

'The private sector felt obliged to do "the right thing" – to pay down debts – which led to the fallacy of composition described. Disastrous consequences were avoided only because the government took the opposite course of action.'[19]

The uniqueness of the 1990s recession in Japan and the 2008 Credit Crunch and subsequent Great Recession lies not in the fact of capitalists suddenly changing their priority from maximising profit to minimising debt. It is more fundamental than that. It is to do with the fact that the economy has entered a unique zone, the critical zone.

THE CLINTON EXPERIMENT

Reflecting on the twin problems facing the Clinton administration upon taking office in 1991 (those of an economic recession coupled with a massive federal debt), Joseph Stiglitz, the then Chairman of President Clinton's Council of Economic Advisors wrote:

---

19. Ibid, p25.

'The president was persuaded that there was a task that had to be attended to first... He had to bring the deficit under control... [But] the theory that has been taught in every course in economics for more than fifty years said that increasing taxes or reducing expenditures in an attempt to reduce the deficit would slow down the economy.

Yet it worked the other way round: 'In the end it turned out that Clinton's strategy for deficit reduction worked. Within a few years, the deficit inherited from the Bush [senior] administration turned into huge surpluses and the economy recovered.'[20]

Stiglitz claims 'the reasons were particular to the 1990s' and asks:

'If deficit reductions in general should have slowed the recovery, to what can we attribute the recovery's vigour? To a sequence of events that was neither expected beforehand nor fully understood as it unfolded. By lowering the deficit, the Clinton administration ended up recapitalising a number of American banks; it was this inadvertent act, as much as anything, that refuelled the economy.'[21]

He puts the success of deficit reduction down to luck; or as he puts it:

---

20. Joseph Stiglitz, *The Roaring Nineties*, Pelican Books, 2003, p36.
21. Ibid, p42.

'Deficit reduction might be described, then, as a lucky mistake – a right decision made for the wrong reasons. And its success rested on another lucky mistake – the Fed's failure to jack up interest rates during the early stages of the recovery as the Fed would surely have done if it hadn't underestimated the recovery strength, just as it had seriously underestimated the force of the decline that preceded it.'[22]

Where does this leave policy making that is based on economic principles and analysis, or is there something more fundamentally different today compared with 40 or 50 years ago? The reality, of course, is that in the US, as in the UK, the underlying terrain of the 1990s was different than that of the 1930s or 1950s. Capital was precariously placed at the edge of the critical zone and, as such, long-cherished economic theories faced the same dismal fate that befell the Phillips Curve among others.[23]

---

22. Ibid, p44.
23. Throughout the 1960s and the best part of the 1970s, the Phillips Curve, named after William Phillips, was taught in every course on economics. William Phillips' theory stated that the lower the unemployment in an economy, the higher the rate of inflation, and consequently all that governments need do to control inflation is to deflate the economy and increase unemployment. The theory was ditched when in the 1970s several economies experienced high levels of both inflation and unemployment simultaneously – what's come to be known as stagflation.

THE CREDIT CRUNCH 2008

The Credit Crunch did not happen by accident, or as a result of greedy bankers and speculators – the modern 'unacceptable face of capitalism'. The financial and economic crisis of 2008 has the same roots as those of the 1970s, namely capital operating at the edge of its critical zone and requiring ever-increasing levels of capital investment and increased pressure on wages.

The Credit Crunch is the result of the combined effect of two inter-related but separate trends: on one hand, the pressure on the rate of profit to fall and, on the other hand, the incessant accumulation of capital.

Capital accumulation (the continuous augmentation of capital by more capital as profits are fed back and reinvested to engender more profit, leading to greater capital accumulation, and so on, in a non-ending cycle of self-expansion) is the inner strength of the capitalist mode of production and its core attraction. But that inner strength, which saw capitalism through cycles of boom and bust, wars, crises, recessions and depressions, is today its core weakness. Its current failure stems from its previous success; its absolute decline from its absolute advance; the greater its success, the worse becomes its predicament. Its reason for existence is the cause of its demise. Capitalism has turned into its opposite – from spewing and utilising abundant capital wealth to choking for lack of it. Welcome to the world of Credit Crunch; capitalism in the critical zone.

To offset this desire for increasing amounts of capital, the same capital is made to circulate at a greater speed, giving the impression of more capital. Overnight investment is just one such example in which capital is invested literally 'overnight' or over a very short period before moving on. The global financial market, together with fast data processing, enables capital to move at a greater speed to more countries, day and night, than ever before. This process is self-generating in the sense that its very success exacerbates the problem. The availability of additional capital as a result of increased circulation drives the cycle towards increased need for more capital in order to counterbalance the fall in the rate of profit, leading to even faster movement of capital, and so on. The slightest interruption will cause problems in the same way as those caused by a slowing car on the M25 in the rush hour.

In the case of global finance, the result of such an interruption is a Credit Crunch. In the case of the 2008 Credit Crunch the interruption in the ever-increasing speed of capital circulation was caused by the failure of sub-prime mortgages, or, to be precise, the recognition of the risk of such mortgages and the overall scale of exposure to these risks. These have come to be known as toxic loans. But this does not make toxic loans the culprit. They were only the trigger and not the cause. The cause is the need for capital to circulate at an ever-faster speed due to its inability to meet the ever-increasing demands of capital.

This is the backdrop of the post-2007 near-meltdown of the global financial/economic system – what the Governor of the

Bank of England described as the biggest crisis since the 1930s, if not ever; launching the biggest ever handover of public money to the financiers.

KEYNES TO THE RESCUE

The 2008 crisis put paid to the love affair with the 'free market' and neo-liberal economic policies, for a time anyway. Not unnaturally, this was seen as a vindication of Keynesian economics, something that lost favour as a consequence of the economic crisis of the 1970s. But neo-liberalism was not a failure; it rescued capitalism from the crisis of the 1970s and, over almost three decades, secured a highly profitable global market.

Keynes believed that ideas govern economic development. He wrote in his famous General Theory of Employment, Interest and Money that 'the ideas of economists and philosophers, both when they are right and when they are wrong, are more powerful than is commonly understood. Indeed the world is ruled by little else'.[24] Keynes set out to temper what he considered to be the 'outstanding faults' of capitalism, 'its failure to provide for full employment and its arbitrary and inequitable distribution of wealth and income'.[25] Keynes finds 'social justifications for significant inadequacies

---

24. John Maynard Keynes, *General Theory*, Harcourt Brace Jovanovich, 1964, p383.
25. Ibid, p372.

of incomes and wealth',[26] and subscribes to the 'traditional advantages of individualism' which, 'if it can be purged from its defects and its abuses, is the best safeguard of personal liberty'.[27]

'Keynes looked forward to the day when economists would have the same status as dentists, as adjusters of minor problems in a well-ordered system.'[28]

As was said earlier, Keynes' solution to a capitalist recession was to reinvigorate the economy with government expenditure. His claim to fame is that he went against the orthodoxy of the time which advocated reduced government borrowing, increased taxation and reduced public expenditure. There is no denying that his approach worked, and for some time Keynesian economics was the accepted view for governments in the UK, US and several other western economies.[29]

Keynes' cure for boom and bust was to balance the propensity to consume with the propensity to invest. The idea is that in a downturn the government stimulates investment through deficit financing of public works, although financing

---

26. Ibid, p373.
27. Ibid, p380.
28. Paul Ormerod, *Death of Economics*, Wiley, 1997, p208.
29. The popularity of Keynesian economics was so widespread that President Nixon is reputed to have said 'we are all Keynesians now', *Time Magazine*, 31 December 1965.

wars and subsequent reconstruction ends up with the same result. Employment will rise and with it demand, to be closely followed by increased private investment and economic recovery. Keynesian economics is reputed to have brought the economy out of the depression of the 1930s, although many contend that it was the Second World War that was the ultimate solution. As stated earlier, Keynesianism was finally abandoned by the Callaghan Labour government with his speech at the Labour Party conference in 1976.

Keynes' remedy is predicated upon the unstated assumption that there is ample capital in private hands to be invested once the propensity to consume has been invigorated. Such an assumption was valid at the time, with capitalism in its conventional zone; but, as we have seen earlier, it is no longer valid as capitalism steers towards the critical zone. Keynes and others never envisaged a situation where the demand for capital is greater than its supply:

'I feel sure that the demand for capital is strictly limited in the sense that it would not be difficult to increase the stock of capital up to a point where its marginal utility has fallen to a very low figure.'[30]

---

30. John Maynard Keynes, *General Theory*, Harcourt Brace Jovanovich, 1964, p375. It is interesting that one of the main pillars of a theory hailed as revolutionary is based on nothing more concrete or scientific than a personal feeling; note Keynes' start to the sentence with 'I feel sure that'.

Keynes maintains that:

'[I]nterest today rewards no genuine sacrifice, any more than does the rent of land. The owner of capital can obtain interest because capital is scarce.'

And taking capital abundance as given, Keynes goes on to advance the aim of:

'an increase in practice (there being nothing in this which is unattainable) in the volume of capital until it ceases to be scarce, so that the functionless investor[31] *will no longer receive a bonus.'*[32]

As the economic recessions from the 1970s onwards have shown, the availability of capital cannot be taken for granted. This is the reason why Keynesian economics floundered. When capital is operating in the conventional zone, a relatively small injection of government-sponsored investment coupled with small fiscal adjustment is all that is needed to stimulate the economy to allow the multiplier to take effect. However, when the economy moves towards the critical zone, a far greater amount of capital injection is needed if capital is to

---

31. By 'functionless investor' Keynes means the 'rentier' – someone who receives interest.
32. John Maynard Keynes, *General Theory*, Harcourt Brace Jovanovich, 1964, p376.

maintain its profitability. Demand for capital, far from being 'strictly limited', is strictly unlimited and almost unsustainable.

Over the past three or four decades there have been several crises, such as the banking crises in Japan and in Brazil in the 1990s. However, the 2008 financial meltdown and the ensuing economic recession is the best example of the insurmountable problems faced by capitalism as it takes its natural course towards the critical zone. Contrary to Keynes' prediction that demand for capital is 'strictly limited', the 2008 crisis proved that capitalism's desire for ever-increasing capital is insatiable, reaching astronomical proportions far in excess of what the market can generate.

In the aftermath of the financial crisis of 2008, bail-outs of £400 billion (in the UK) and $700 billion (in the US) were advanced to prevent complete collapse of the system. More, much more, will be needed to keep capitalism afloat. The bail-outs were accompanied by quantitative easing (printing money). Such giveaways ultimately, directly or indirectly, come out of the pockets of the working population, hence the austerity measures imposed by governments in the UK, US and other nations.

Four years after the 2008 crash, the bail-out continues with trillions poured into the financial structures as politicians attempt to avoid sovereign debt defaults.[33] It is like a patient who, in order to survive, requires a regular injection of new

---

33. In the European Union, an anticipated bail-out for Italy alone (December 2011) is estimated at €1.4tn.

blood. Blood transfusions may save the recipient, but it will ultimately kill the donor. So it is with capitalism, in its need for increased amounts of capital injections on a regular and frequent basis. Such transference of wealth from the working population may save the recipients, but it will ultimately emaciate the donors.

CHAPTER 7

Post-Capitalist Economy

Just as the embryo of capitalism, commodity production, was present in the pre-capitalist economy, so the embryo of the post-capitalist mode of production is present in today's highly developed mode of production. All the elements for a post-capitalist economy (to one degree or another) are present within the capitalist system itself. In an advanced capitalist system, these elements are fully matured and poised to take over. So what is the new economic system that is to replace capitalism? What is the post-capitalist mode of production?

In investigating the likely shape of a post-capitalist economy, it is more fruitful to start by defining what it would not be and gradually move on to explore what it could be, how it could operate and how, in such a system, environmental issues (which under capitalism are treated as a specialised discipline, tangential to the process of resource allocation) would become an integral part of the process of economic planning.

With an economy in which commodities are produced for the sole purpose of exchange – commonly known as the market economy – universally regarded as the natural mode of production and exchange, it is hard to imagine a non-commodity system of production. Historically, far from being the natural mode of production that has existed 'throughout human history',[1] an economic system based on commodity production is a relatively recent development. Up to the Industrial Revolution, the production of commodities for exchange was economically insignificant, and where it existed it was incidental to the economy as a whole.[2] If the capitalist system of commodity production were to end, the law of value (the defining feature of capitalism) would disappear with it. It thus follows that a post-capitalist mode of production would be a non-commodity mode of production – one in which the law of value which underpins and regulates the commodity mode of production has no further relevance or application, in the same way as Newton's laws of mechanics have no application in the world of quantum physics.

The process of moving from a capitalist to a fully fledged post-capitalist economy would entail a transfer phase – an

1. Stuart L Hart, *Capitalism at the Crossroads*, Wharton School Publishing, 2007, p42.
2. 'The mode of production in which the product takes the form of a commodity, or is produced directly for exchange, is the most general and most embryonic form of bourgeois production. It therefore makes its appearance at an early date in history, though not in the same predominating and characteristic manner as now-a-days', Karl Marx, *Capital*, Volume 1, Ch 1, para 138.

overlapping phase in which commodity production might persist in parts of the economy, on a scale which in highly advanced economies (like those of the US and the UK) would be relatively tiny, as the process of evolution took its course. Furthermore, this chapter will show that under the non-commodity production mode, looking after the environment would become an integral part of the production process.

The conventional alternative to capitalism is commonly known as a socialist economy based on need and not profit. However, the term 'socialism' has been so misrepresented and abused that it has almost lost all of its original meaning. For a glimpse of the future, we have to go back to fundamentals.

HOW DID WE GET TO WHERE WE ARE TODAY?

As explained in Chapter 4, things have been exchanged ever since the first human social gatherings, initially for other things (barter) and later for money. However, only under the capitalist mode of production are things, all things, as a general rule, made for the sole purpose of exchange, in what is known as commodity production.[3] Once commodity production

---

3. 'There have been a great variety of societies in which products are exchanged and thereby acquire the form of commodities. Yet if the products have been produced for a different purpose, that of satisfying the producers' and others' needs and wants, they have not been produced as commodities', Andrew Kliman, *Reclaiming Marx's Capital*, Lexington Books, 2007, p20.

takes hold, the exchange value or price[4] of commodities is determined by the law of value.

The law of value states that the value of a commodity is determined by the labour time embodied in it, and when commodities are exchanged, they are exchanged as equivalents.[5] Barter, the elementary form of expressing the relative values of two articles, is an exchange of use values. Marx traces the first step made by an object of utility towards acquiring exchange value back to 'when [the object] forms a non-use-value for its owner, and that happens when it forms a superfluous portion of some article required for his immediate wants. The exchange of commodities, therefore, first begins on the boundaries of communities, at their points of contact with other similar communities, or with members of the latter'. He goes on:

'So soon, however, as products once become commodities in the external relations of a community, they also, by reaction,

---

4. While the exchange value of a commodity is the amount of what Marx calls 'socially necessary labour' to produce it. Socially necessary labour is the average amount of labour required to produce a commodity in any given state of economic and technological development. Price on the other hand is the actual amount of money received through a sale in the open market. The two may or may not be identical. For our immediate purposes, exchange value and price are treated as the same.

5. 'They contain the value of a certain quantity of labour which we exchange for what is supposed at the time to contain the value of an equal quantity', Adam Smith, *The Wealth of Nations*, Penguin, 1979, p133.

become so in its internal intercourse. The proportions in which they are exchangeable are at first quite a matter of chance. What makes them exchangeable is the mutual desire of their owners to alienate them. Meantime the need for foreign objects of utility gradually establishes itself. The constant repetition of exchange makes it a normal social act. In the course of time, therefore, some portion at least of the products of labour must be produced with a special view to exchange. From that moment the distinction becomes firmly established between the utility of an object for the purposes of consumption, and its utility for the purposes of exchange. Its use-value becomes distinguished from its exchange value.'[6]

But commodity exchange as such does not of necessity create surplus value and, with it, the capitalist system of production. For this to happen, an individual producer must hire an extra hand to work for him, to sell his labour power for a wage; in other words, labour power must be transformed into a commodity.

POST-CAPITALISM AND PRIVATE/PUBLIC OWNERSHIP

Once labour power becomes a commodity it acquires a value, an exchange value measured by the labour time socially necessary for its reproduction. However, the labour time

---

6. Marx, *Capital*, Volume 1, Ch 2, para 7.

socially necessary for the reproduction of labour power need not be, and as a rule is not, the same as the labour time the worker is contracted to work; in fact it is far less. The difference is surplus value, a value added to the commodity by that proportion of the labour time that the employer who hires the labour power does not pay for. Surplus value is an integral part of the law of value in a commodity mode of production; it is a direct outcome of the relations of production of an economic system based on the production of goods for the sole purpose of exchange in which the means of production are privately owned.

Take a case where every individual owns all the means of production. In such a hypothetical situation, every individual would be able to produce articles for their own use and there would be no need to purchase them. There would be no question of exchange. These articles cannot be categorised as commodities; they are items produced for use, having use value to their owners. Commodity production, production for the sole purpose of exchange, would cease. Social ownership of the means of production, the societal manifestation of each individual owning all means of production, is, therefore, a prerequisite for a non-commodity mode of production.

POST-CAPITALISM AND VALUE

In a non-commodity production system, things, items, articles and products still have value, in the sense that they are valuable, but it is not the exchange value of a commodity in a commodity mode of production. Use values have no relation to exchange value. Consider Adam Smith's example of air, which is a life necessity, being free – yet a luxury like a cut diamond, with no practical use, commanding a very high exchange value. In a post-capitalist economy, products and services could be assigned a utility score which might or might not correspond to the individual labour time necessary for their production.[7]

The law of value plays the central role in the development of the capitalist mode of production and, in doing so, it drives two opposing trends. It brings down wages at one end and pays high wages for newly developed skills at the other. The fast-changing processes in the commercial, industrial and service sectors require not just a highly skilled workforce, but one with highly transferrable skills. In the early stages of capitalism, illiteracy was common, as it is today in developing nations.[8] Far from the small repetitive tasks required in a Victorian cotton mill, a Ford car production line or a typing pool, today the vast majority of wage earners in an advanced capitalist country like Britain are involved in skilled occupations requiring a varying degree of education and training. In advanced economies, a minimum level of literacy and numeracy, not to mention computer literacy, is essential, even for the most unskilled job. In the UK in 2011, 71% of all

---

7. However, the totality of utility scores would have to equal the totality of labour time expended in production by society as a whole.
8. India (in 2011) has an illiteracy rate of 25%.

occupations are highly skilled (including 25% being managers, teachers and engineers, and 27% being technicians and administrative workers), 15% are medium-skilled occupations such as farmers, welders and child carers, and only 12% are low-skilled occupations, what the Office for National Statistics calls 'elementary' occupations, such as farm workers and traffic wardens.

Hand in hand with the increased skilling of the workforce is the disappearance of the narrow scope of 'job-for-life' occupations. In their place we have the development of a more rounded individual worker. Capitalism goes full circle: from the alienation of the Industrial Revolution, the dehumanisation of the division of labour, and the de-skilling of the conveyer belt, to its opposite, with the dignity of a highly skilled workforce, the breakdown of the division of labour and the emergence of the rounded individual;[9] in a word: proletarian professionalism – the spectre that haunts developed economies today. Capitalism thus lays the grounds for its succeeding system.

PROLETARIAN PROFESSIONALISM

On one hand, at its beginning, capitalism removed the 'halo' that shrouded the professional occupations and drove them

---

9. Division of labour is not the same as specialisation. The latter increases understanding and skill in a particular subject while the former reduces work to its most basic tasks that require little skill or no skill to perform.

into the arms of the proletariat.[10] On the other hand, at its most developed stage, it raises the proletariat to the status of the professional.[11] Proletarian professionalism is thus born, bringing with it a new contradiction between the dignity and self-respect of the professional health worker, scientist, engineer, tool maker, miner, chemical worker, and artist, on one hand, and the intellectually deadening commercial demands of profit-seeking corporations on the other.

Together with the skilled workforce comes pride – pride in one's self, pride in one's occupation and pride in the product. This is in direct contrast to governments' belief that the only incentive is a monetary one. In the UK, governments'

---

10. 'The bourgeoisie has stripped of its halo every occupation hitherto honoured and looked up to with reverent awe. It has converted the physician, the lawyer, the priest, the poet, the man of science, into its paid wage labourers', Marx and Engels, *Communist Manifesto*, 1848.

11. 'Modern Industry, on the other hand, through its catastrophes imposes the necessity of recognising, as a fundamental law of production, variation of work, consequently fitness of the labourer for varied work, consequently the greatest possible development of his varied aptitudes. It becomes a question of life and death for society to adapt the mode of production to the normal functioning of this law. Modern Industry, indeed, compels society, under penalty of death, to replace the detail-worker of to-day, crippled by life-long repetition of one and the same trivial operation, and thus reduced to the mere fragment of a man, by the fully developed individual, fit for a variety of labours, ready to face any change of production, and to whom the different social functions he performs, are but so many modes of giving free scope to his own natural and acquired powers', Marx, *Capital*, Volume 1, Ch 15, para 139.

obsession with setting targets for the NHS, for instance, reflects their belief that professional nurses and doctors would shirk their responsibilities to patients but for the threat of financial penalties. In Britain, the Blair/Brown government was so keen on divesting doctors of their professionalism that, under a new contract in 2003, GPs were given extra money to provide services such as contraception and vaccination which the majority were already providing.[12] 'As Dr Crippen, the anonymous author of the NHS Blog Doctor site, put it: "The really high-achieving entrepreneurial GPs do not waste time seeing patients. They employ others to do that ... the extra money has been earned by hitting government targets [which] have little to do with health care, but a lot to do with "process" and bogus but quantifiable "healthcare achievements".'[13]

In developing countries, manual jobs such as street cleaning and factory work are considered menial, not deserving of respect. In developed countries, all jobs are treated with respect and all workers with dignity. This is the first thing that anyone coming from a developing country notices; the cleaner and the gardener are treated with respect in the same way as the office worker and the teacher. All are respected regardless of the job they do. At some stage, technological advance reaches such a level that the scope for unskilled labour (what the Office for National Statistics categorise as 'elementary occupations') almost disappears. The alienation that Marx talked about, which capitalism wishes to enforce, turns into its opposite.

---

12. David Batty, *Guardian*, 3 March 2003.
13. Nick Cohen, *Observer*, 31 December 2006.

Professionalism was formed in the womb of the capitalist mode of production at the same time as socialised production comprehensively encompassed the economy. The two trends, which developed simultaneously, lay the foundation of the post-capitalist mode of production, a non-commodity mode of production.[14] 'A spectre is haunting Europe – the spectre of Communism.' Thus began the *Communist Manifesto* some 150 years ago. Today the spectre is in a different guise – no less 'dangerous', but more advanced, more subtle. It is professionalism.

THE NHS – A CASE OF NON-COMMODITY ECONOMY

Apart from the general principles that underlie a non-commodity economy, it would be sterile to draw a blueprint for it, to prescribe in detail what it would look like. However, instances where whole economic entities function, to a large extent, outside the commodity-producing sector, could give us a glimpse of a post-capitalist society. One such example is the NHS, or to be precise, the pre-reform NHS. The NHS, with its large and comprehensive scope, functions as a small economy. The NHS 'so radically eliminated market

---

14. '... and new, higher relations of production never appear before the material conditions of their existence have matured in the womb of the old society itself' wrote Marx in the Preface to a contribution to the *Critique of Political Economy* (selected works), Foreign Language Publishing House, Moscow, Volume 1, p363.

mechanism within the system (with the exception of external suppliers and private patients) there was no invoicing and so no payments of bills'.[15] It provides us with the best example of a non-commodity post-capitalist economy, not just because of its public service ethos, but because it encompasses some of the highest professional skills.

In his excellent book, the *Political Economy of Health Care*, Julian Tudor Hart looks at the history of the NHS and gives an insight of its modus operandi. Soon after the formation of the NHS, attempts were made to undermine and dismantle it. He observes:

> *'As early as 1952, it was argued that 'Medical care being in constant and universal demand, and commanding high prices from those able to pay, at zero price demand must reach infinity, and soon bankrupt the service. [This] was echoed in cabinet by Stafford Cripps, then by Hugh Gaitskell, Attlee's Chancellors of the Exchequer. [This] view was reinforced by Conservative Minister of Health, Enoch Powell and finally set in stone by Allan Williams as the foundation of his York school of health economics. Despite the apparently self-evident logic of theory, the hard fact remained that for more than three decades the NHS not only existed, but seemed to deliver a service comparable with or better than any other developed economy, at a lower cost than most of them, and, at less than half the per capita cost of care in the US, where the system*

---

15. Allyson Pollock, *NHS PLC*, Verso, 2005, p17.

was least socially inclusive and most exposed to market choice and competition.'[16]

Julian Tudor Hart gives three reasons why this was the case. Firstly, demand was not infinite, but more or less reflected the burdens of ill health and public expectations of what could be done to relieve it. Secondly, bulk central purchasing greatly reduced the cost of many NHS consumptions, most obviously of pharmaceutical products. Thirdly, because the NHS was what Julian Tudor Hart calls an 'internally cash-free, gift economy', it was spared the huge bureaucratic burdens weighing on all commercial undertakings.

The cash-free economy of the NHS was responsible for more than just a highly efficient delivery of health care. It created a new culture, as Hart goes on to explain: 'Within always inadequate global budgets, different hospital departments got for themselves as much as they could justify to managements operating by consensus, relying on professional prestige, and partly on advancing scientific evidence.' This culture, Hart notes:

'contained within itself an embryonic economy geared to human needs rather than profit, always seeking expression, and continually reinforced by the generally humane and socially intelligent orientation of advances in knowledge.'[17]

---

16. Julian Tudor Hart, *The Political Economy of Health Care*, Policy Press, 2006, p26.
17. Ibid, p29.

It was of course far more than a cash-free internal economy; it was a non-commodity economy in which, as Hart points out, 'staff time became the effective currency', an economy where, internally, the labour law of value did not operate. It should, therefore, not come as a surprise that when he asked for the cost of the work done, 'nobody in our X-ray departments or pathology laboratories knew the cost of anything they did'. He goes on:

> *'Unit directors of radiography and pathology knew about their global budgets, and necessarily worked within them, but cost of items of service varied enormously according to throughput and how close to maximum capacity staff and machines were working, needing reserve capacity for workloads varying between wide limits from time to time. They were concerned to balance their books – not to spend more than they got to spend from hospital administration – but they had no interest in making a profit, only in providing a service. As both departments had hugely improved their service to GP users over the previous 20 years, motivation was evidently good, but was not prompted by hopes of profit.'*[18]

When he stressed that he needed to know unit costs of, for example, the consequences of ordering a chest X-ray or full blood count, no one could give a meaningful answer 'because in their terms, this was not a meaningful question' and that's

---

18. Ibid, p30.

because none of these activities was treated as a commodity[19] and, as such, could not be allocated an exchange value or price in accordance with the labour law of value. Furthermore, internally within the NHS, labour power itself was no longer treated as a commodity and, as such, did not have an exchange value or price. That being so, the only measure left is labour time, the currency of a non-commodity economy. It isn't that the NHS is 'an alternative model for production of value, of non-commodity wealth', as Julian Tudor Hart puts it;[20] rather it is a model of non-commodity, non-exchange-value production. It is precisely because health services are not commodities they do not acquire an exchange value; they have a utility, a use value, only.

NON-COMMODITY PRODUCTION AND THE ENVIRONMENT

Under the non-commodity mode of production, looking after the environment would become an integral part of the production process. In the same way as parents avoid anything that hinders the future development of their offspring, the non-commodity economy would do nothing that hindered a continued safe and sustainable environment. What parent

---

19. 'The integration within the NHS system depended on the rejection of the idea of health care as a commodity', Allyson Pollock, *NHS PLC*, Verso, 2005, p17.
20. Julian Tudor Hart, *The Political Economy of Health Care*, Policy Press, 2006, p235.

would deny a baby adequate milk to sustain the baby's growth in order to satisfy their desire for alcohol? There may be the odd individual that does that, but as a society we see it as abhorrent and unacceptable.

All of the 'solutions' offered by the environmentalists – from self-denial to low growth, etc – that required persuasion, regulation or legislation under commodity production would become second nature in a non-commodity economy. The issue of 'discounting the future' doesn't even arise.

Discounting is a quintessentially capitalist concept in which future benefits of, say, reducing CO_2 emissions are translated into a monetary value at today's prices. It is based on the idea that an amount of money is worth more in 12 months than it is now, on the assumption that if it is placed in an interest-bearing account it would be augmented by the interest accrued. Thus, given an interest rate of 5%, to raise £100 in one year's time, £95.23, known as the discounted present value, has to be put away today: £100/1.05 = £95.23. For two years, the figure is £100/(1.05)^2 = £90.70, over 10 years it is £100/(1.05)^{10} = £61.39, and over 50 years it is an insignificant £8.72. The interest rate over the discounted period is called the discount rate, which is based on current and estimated interest rates in the future. This is the method used in cost–benefit analysis by corporations and governments, including an appraisal of environmental schemes. As can be seen, the longer the discounting period, the smaller is the discounted present value. Thus for schemes such as forestation and reducing CO_2

emissions (which take a long time to produce results and show benefit), the discounted value is very small.

'The conspicuous example is forestry... In this case the benefit of a tree that takes 50 years to grow appears to be reduced to comparative insignificance in terms of present values.'[21]

In the non-capitalist world, say in a family, future benefits for one's offspring are given a higher value than present gratification, otherwise how can you explain parents needing to save to put their children through university.

That is not to say that there may not be a conflict between long-term sustainability and contemporary needs. Take the example of the parents making a choice between feeding the baby with milk or spending the money on wine for themselves. In this case, the choice is clear. However, if it was a matter of a choice between baby's milk and potatoes to feed themselves, the choice may not be that clear cut. For if they don't feed themselves, they would die and there would be no one left to care for the baby. Compromises have to be made. That is not discounting the future; it is ensuring a future. Under non-commodity production, renewability and sustainability would, for the first time, be integrated into every aspect of the economy.

---

21. DW Pearce, et al, *Blueprint for a Green Economy*, Earthscan, 1996, p137.

Chapter 8

Capitalism versus Planet Earth – An Irreconcilable Conflict

On 25 August 2011, a British team became the first to row to the North Magnetic Pole, a feat that would have been impossible only a decade or so ago. Rowing to the pole in an open boat became possible because climate change has meant that the Arctic ice sheet has retreated a record distance in the last 30 years. Jock Wishart, the team leader, said that it was obvious from looking out of the boat that a lot of the ice has disappeared from areas that a few years ago would have been frozen over.[1] This is a cause for concern, because if melting polar ice were to release fresh water southward into the North Atlantic at a fast enough rate, it could alter the Gulf Stream's route.

The break-up of the ice sheets is also opening the region to oil and gas exploration as well as providing a new shipping route between the Atlantic and Pacific Oceans for supertankers

---

1. *Independent on Sunday*, 27 August 2011.

and giant cargo ships, introducing new pollutants and accelerating the threat of global warming. This is an early glimpse of our planet in the not-so-distant future.

Similar developments are taking place all over the globe. The *Guardian's* Head of Environment, Damian Carrington, put it this way: 'It is now clear that the planet's problems are systemic... [g]lobal warming, crashing biodiversity and food, land and water shortages.'[2] Thus, barely 200 years into the Anthropocene epoch, planet Earth is approaching an environmental tipping point.

The start of the newly defined Anthropocene is correlated with the birth of capitalism, the invention of the steam engine and the dawn of the Industrial Revolution. This is not a coincidence. Neither is it a coincidence that an environmental tipping point should be reached at the same time as capitalism faces its greatest financial and economic crisis, the uniqueness of which is belatedly being acknowledged. The UK's Prime Minister, David Cameron, speaking at his party conference in October 2011, said:

'People understand that when the economy goes into recession, times get tough. But normally, after a while, things pick up. Strong growth returns. People get back into work. This time, it's not like that. And people want to know why the good times are so long coming. The answer is straightforward, but uncomfortable. This was no normal recession.'

---

2. *Guardian*, The Greens' Midlife Move, 14 September 2011.

The next day, launching the UK's second tranche of £75 billion worth of quantitative easing, Mervyn King, the Governor of the Bank of England, told *Channel 4 News*: 'This is undoubtedly the biggest financial crisis the world has ever faced and it has continued now for four years.' A month later, UK unemployment recorded its highest level for 17 years, with youth unemployment at a record 1.2 million, prompting the media to talk of a 'lost generation'. By the end of November 2011, the UK Chancellor of the Exchequer, George Osborne, made it clear in his Autumn Statement to the House of Commons that the crisis promises to be deeper and more prolonged than anything since the 1930s,[3] while Martin Wolf of the *Financial Times* talked of a 'lost decade'.[4]

We are constantly being told that the solution to this unprecedented financial crisis that is gripping the globe is austerity, long-term austerity. In the UK, even before the austerity measures announced in the March 2011 budget had been implemented, a further austerity package was announced in November 2011. A report from the Institute for Fiscal Studies shows that household income is expected to fall by an average of 7.4% between 2009–10 and 2012–13, with real median household incomes being lower in 2015–16 than they were in 2002–03. According to the Institute for Fiscal Studies (IFS), around 100,000 will be added to the number of

---

3. *Financial Times*, 30 November 2011.
4. Ibid.

children in poverty during 2012–13 alone.[5] 'There have been periods in Britain's history – the famine of the 1340s, followed by the Black Death', remarked Larry Elliott of the *Guardian*, 'when there were colossal falls in living standards, but what the IFS described yesterday has no precedent in modern history.'[6] The age of austerity has begun, but when will it end?

A DOUBLE WHAMMY

As efforts are made to extricate the economy from its crisis, environmental considerations take a back seat, and governments, who see their first priority as saving the economy, turn a blind eye to corporate pollution and, where they exist, dilute or remove environmental regulations. At times of crisis, regulations that protect the environment are seen as 'piling costs on the energy bills of households and companies'.[7] In his 2011 Autumn Statement, George Osborne described green policies as a 'ridiculous cost' to British business and warned against burdening business with 'endless social and environmental goals' as he 'gave £250m worth of assistance and rebates to the most energy intensive companies,

---

5. Institute for Fiscal Studies, 1 November 2011.
6. *Guardian*, 1 December 2011.
7. 'Now we know that a decade of environmental laws and regulations are piling costs on the energy bills of households and companies', Chancellor of the Exchequer, George Osborne, speaking at Conservative Party Conference, October 2011.

announced a massive road-building scheme and hinted at watering down regulations protecting British wildlife'.[8]

The planet faces a double whammy: an environmental meltdown and an economic crisis, the like of which has never been experienced. The one feeds the other, and both are poised at the edge of a vortex. A stark choice faces humanity: save the planet and ditch capitalism, or save capitalism and ditch the planet. Capitalists and political leaders have made up their minds: 'We're not going to save the planet by putting our country out of business,'[9] declared George Osborne, and he is not alone. The inhabitants of Easter Island had no choice. To save themselves they had to destroy the very environment their livelihood depended on. We, on the other hand, have a choice; the question is will we take it?

SAVE THE PLANET – REDUCE GREENHOUSE GAS EMISSIONS

It was Dr James E Hansen, Director of NASA's Institute for Space Studies in Manhattan, who in 1988 told the US Senate Energy and Natural Resources Committee that it was 99% certain that the global warming trend was not a natural variation but was caused by a build-up of CO_2 and other gases in the atmosphere. He said 'It is time to stop waffling so much and say that the evidence is pretty strong that the greenhouse

---

8. *Guardian*, 29 November 2011.
9. Chancellor George Osborne speaking at Conservative Party Conference, October 2011.

effect is here' and called for a broad national and international programme to slow the pace of global warming. A gauntlet was thrown down to the international community: control greenhouse gases or risk climate change that poses a real threat to human life. While this was not the first intervention that placed environmental issues on the international agenda, it was the most dramatic to date.

Long before, in 1972, the UN had held a Conference on the Human Environment which put the environment on the international agenda for the first time. By 1983, the impact of economic development on the environment had become the subject of an inquiry by the UN World Commission on Environment and Development, known as the Brundtland Commission, after its chair Gro Harlem Brundtland.

Thus began the era of international activity to bring about a global collaboration for a low-carbon, low-polluting global economy. Optimism reigned as the United Nations Environment Programme (UNEP) and the World Meteorological Organization (WMO) established the Intergovernmental Panel on Climate Change (IPCC) in December 1988 to provide the world with a clear scientific view of the current state of knowledge about climate change and its potential environmental and socioeconomic impacts. The first IPCC Assessment Report was produced in 1990. It established climate change and its consequences as a topic deserving serious political consideration. The IPCC's supplementary report of 1992 played a decisive role in the creation of the United Nations Framework Convention on

Climate Change (UNFCCC), the key international treaty to reduce global warming and cope with the consequences of climate change.

In 1992 the Rio de Janeiro Earth Summit was held, with over 100 heads of state and heads of government attending. Furthermore, the UN established the UN Commission on Sustainable Development (CSD), which monitors and guides implementation of the Rio commitments. It was followed five years later by the Earth Summit +5 special session of the UN General Assembly at which governments agreed a programme of action to further implement the agenda of the Earth Summit. In the same year, the Third Conference of the Parties to the UNFCCC was held in Kyoto, Japan, on 1–12 December 1997.

Optimism was high. The first global agreement on action to reduce greenhouse gas emissions, the Kyoto Protocol was negotiated at the 1997 conference and came into force in February 2005. Richer countries, known as 'Annex 1 countries', were subject to legally binding emissions reduction targets. In aggregate, these cuts seek a minimum 5% reduction in the 1990 level of all Annex 1 countries' emissions before the end of the first commitment period in 2012. However, the US refused to ratify the protocol, and Canada and Japan have largely disregarded their Kyoto commitments. Furthermore, the detailed rules not only exclude emissions from aviation and shipping but also contain various loopholes. These shortcomings have allowed global emissions to mushroom. By 2009 they were 40% above the 1990 baseline, and the concentration of CO_2 in the atmosphere is now at its highest level for at least the last 800,000 years.[10]

The secretariat of the UNFCCC has been engaged for some years in seeking agreement to renew the Kyoto Protocol. In the 2007 Bali Action Plan, the Annex 1 countries acknowledged their legal obligation to negotiate a second commitment period from 2012, the US agreed to participate in a comparable and parallel negotiating track, and the emerging economies agreed to reduce their trajectories of emissions growth, subject to financial and technical support.

SUBSEQUENT CONFERENCES

The three subsequent UNFCCC annual conferences have witnessed a gradual retreat by the richer countries from the Bali Action Plan. Japan and Russia have openly opposed renewal of the Kyoto Protocol and Canada has withdrawn from it. They wanted to abandon the UNFCCC principle of a global mitigation target based on science, divided up by agreement between countries and enforced by legal agreement. Instead, they advocated a 'pledge and review' system in which countries offer independent targets according to their circumstances. The problem with this softer approach is that the pledges add up to barely half the reductions recommended by scientists.[11] The 2007 Fourth Assessment Report of the

---

10. www.uk.oneworld.net/guides/climatechange.
11. One World, Climate Change and Poverty, 2011.

Intergovernmental Panel on Climate Change (IPCC) advised that cuts of 25–40% by 2020 would be necessary to limit average temperature rise to 2°C – the threshold beyond which there will be 'catastrophic and irreversible' climate change. Efforts to persuade key countries to improve their pledges in order to fill the 'emissions gap' have so far failed. All eyes were on the UN climate conference held in Durban in December 2011.

With expectation very low, following the debacle in Copenhagen two years earlier and in Cancún in 2010, any agreement at Durban was going to be hailed as a great victory: 'After Copenhagen and Cancún, it seemed implausible that rich and poor nations would ever agree that they would one day strike a legally binding treaty, but they have,' wrote George Monbiot in his blog. He went on: 'That doesn't mean that the outcome was good: even if everything happens as planned, we are still likely to end up with more than 2°C of warming, which threatens great harm to many of the world's people and places.' Michael Jacobs, Visiting Professor in the Grantham Research Institute on Climate Change and the Environment at the London School of Economics, endorsed the low expectations and summarised its positive outcome as follows:

'First, it has forced countries to admit that their current climate policies are inadequate. The Durban agreement explicitly refers to the "emissions gap" – the difference between the aggregate impact of commitments that countries have made, and the upper limit of emissions required to have a

chance of meeting the globally agreed goal of no more than two degrees of global warming.

Second, Durban has re-established the principle that climate change should be tackled through a framework of international law. Since the failure of the Copenhagen talks two years ago, it seemed that the world had abandoned this ideal in favour of so-called "pledge and review", in which countries made purely voluntary national commitments.

At the heart of the Durban deal is the extension of the Kyoto Protocol, the legally binding treaty signed in 1997. Although only the EU and a few other countries are likely to maintain their commitment to it.

Durban has drawn up a roadmap towards a new treaty to succeed Kyoto in 2020, which for the first time will require the big emerging economies such as China, India and Brazil, to also make legally binding commitments.

Third, the conference has established a new Green Climate Fund which, if properly financed (still an "if" not a "when"), will provide vital support to the poorest countries to reduce their emissions and adapt to the climate change they are already experiencing.'

But these commitments fall far short of what is required, as Bill Hare, Director at Climate Action Tracker, explained: 'There are still no new pledges on the table and the process agreed in Durban towards raising the ambition and increasing emission reductions is uncertain in its outcome.' Andy Atkins, Executive Director of Friends of the Earth, said: 'This empty shell of a plan leaves the planet hurtling towards catastrophic climate change.'[12]

Surely, with such compelling evidence about the dangers of global warming, and in view of the engagement of the UN, the world's political leaders would reach agreement on measures to halt the increase in greenhouse gas emissions in time to save the planet. The Montreal Protocol for the protection of the ozone layer is hailed as an example of international cooperation on an environmental threat that lay beyond the confines of any one country or government. Oliver Tickell explains:

'The most effective international treaty for controlling greenhouse gas emission to date is the Montreal Protocol on Substances that Deplete the Ozone Layer. The Montreal Protocol which came into force in 1 January 1989 uses on a "direct regulation" approach to phase out the production of [chlorofluorocarbons – CFCs] responsible for depleting the atmospheric ozone that protects the Earth's surface from dangerous UV-B radiation, with timetables set for each chemical. It gave [developing] countries more time to comply and created a Multinational Fund with some US$2bn to invest in technology transfer to help the [developing] countries achieve their targets. The Montreal Protocol has been highly effective.'[13]

---

12. *Guardian*, 12 December 2011.
13. Oliver Tickell, *Kyoto 2*, Zed Books, 2008, p52.

Tickell goes on to observe that '[t]he relatively easy and rapid success of the Montreal Protocol stands in stark contrast to the slow, meagre and expensive gains achieved under the Kyoto Protocol'.[14] This raises the question, why hasn't Kyoto followed the same path as Montreal?

MONTREAL VERSUS KYOTO

When discussing the 'polluter pays' tax in Chapter 5, we noted that when the production cost of a product or service is increased, for example through a pollution tax, the rate of profit for producers of that product or service falls, but also that if these products and services constitute a small part of the national economy, the average rate of profit of the economy at large is unaffected. We saw how in the short term, the extra cost is shared out between the producers of these products and services and their customers. However, in a relatively short period of time, the rate of profit of the producers of the affected products goes back to the prevailing average. In this case, the extra cost (the pollution tax in our example) is borne by the customer in full. However, if the pollution tax is a universal one, affecting all products, such as a tax on energy use, then its introduction will lead to a drop in the rate of profit of all producers. That being the case, the average rate of profit will fall.

---

14. Ibid, p54.

The Montreal Protocol related to the former category of products that constituted a small part of the overall economy. It committed governments to require producers who used CFCs to replace them with substitutes which were more expensive. This constituted an extra cost to a small part of the economy, namely those enterprises that used CFCs. Furthermore, those engaged in manufacturing CFCs were compensated and helped in producing substitutes. The average rate of profit of the economy was not affected and the cost of phasing out CFCs was thus ultimately borne by consumers.

When it comes to the much more comprehensive measures needed to tackle climate change it is, of course, a very different matter. In this case, additional expenditure resulting from implementing measures to protect the environment – such as setting a regulatory programme for greenhouse gas emissions, bringing an end to coal-burning power plants and protecting forests and other natural ecosystems – is not limited to one category of product but will affect all products. In this situation, the effect, as we have seen, will be to lower the average rate of profit across the economy as a whole.

The falling rate of profit by itself is not a problem (see Chapter 4). Capitalism has coped with falling rates of profit since its very inception. It has always managed to increase profits regardless of the fall in the rate of profit by expanding total capital outlay, which, with capital in the conventional or classical zone, has been accomplished with relative case. The question is – and here is the rub – can capitalism at its current stage of development afford a further fall in its rate of profit?

When capitalism was operating in the conventional zone, with relatively low capital investment and relatively high rates of profit, a fall in the rate of profit was compensated for by increased capital outlay resulting in increased profits. This is no longer possible when capital is operating in the critical zone, which, as we have seen in Chapter 4, is where the UK and other advanced capitalist economies are today. When operating in the critical zone, the necessary increase in capital outlay to compensate for a fall in the rate of profit is prohibitively large, and profits tumble.

The irony is that, when capital was in the conventional zone, it would have been able to take measures to protect the global environment, but it did not need to or at least there was no general awareness of the need to. Today, when the global environment is in dire need of protection, capital operating in the critical zone is unable to take steps to provide any such protection. As a result, we have the vicious circle of capital continually expanding and, in the process, polluting the atmosphere, rivers and oceans, and depleting natural resources in one region and then moving on to another; and so on, in a cycle of expansion–exploitation–pollution. Thus, as capitalism approaches its tipping point, so does the planet.

ARE POLITICIANS TO BLAME?

It is tempting to blame political leaders for the failure to enact measures to protect the planet against global warming. David Cameron is blamed for going back on his promise to lead 'the greenest government ever' and Barack Obama for his obstructive approach to the 2012 Durban conference. But politicians are constrained by economic considerations. They may have some good intentions of taking action on behalf of the environment, but far more powerful is the economic logic of the capitalist system of production.

It isn't that leaders find 'persuading Europeans and Americans that they should tolerate nearly a decade of austerity, a daunting challenge', or that political leaders 'have no language in which to convey the importance and urgency of what needs to be done',[15] for they seemed to manage it with remarkable ease when it came to saving financial and economic systems. Witness the aplomb with which Chancellor of the Exchequer George Osborne announced a decade of severe austerity for the UK in his 2011 Autumn Statement to the House of Commons. The reason why politicians such as Osborne shy away from taking similar measures to protect the environment is because their priority is not saving the planet but saving capitalism. Their aim is not sustainable development but sustainable capitalism.

A NEW DIMENSION

In the eurozone, the financial/economic crisis has an added dimension: sovereign debt. The debts of some Member States, such as Ireland, Greece and Italy, form such a large percentage

---

15. Peter Wilby, *Guardian*, 3 December 2011.

of their respective GDPs (sometimes even exceeding them) that financial markets moved to downgrade their credit rating, which hugely increased the cost of borrowing to pay off outstanding debts. To prevent a default and the prospect of European and other banks losing part or all of the money they had lent out to these countries (what is referred to as 'taking a hair cut'), a massive bail-out was hastily arranged by other EU states, notably Germany.

Apart from the austerity measures that the people of these indebted nations have had imposed on them in return for the bail-outs, their very sovereignty is compromised, democratic processes subverted and parliamentary accountability all-but demolished. In Ireland the Taoiseach, Brian Cowen, had to resign following popular opposition to the austerity measures demanded by the EU and the IMF as a condition of the €85 billion bail-out agreed in November 2010. However, instead of calling an immediate general election, Cowen continued in office and, with the help of the 'opposition', got the austerity measures through the Dail before the Irish people had a chance to vote, rendering the subsequent general election all-but meaningless, as the austerity measures which caused the government to fall could not figure as an issue in the general election. In Greece, a referendum on the austerity measures demanded by the eurozone and the IMF proposed by Prime Minister George Papandreou so outraged the bankers that he was forced to retract and resign. He was replaced by Lucas Papademos, a former European Central Bank Vice-president who has never been elected. Similarly, with Italy, discredited

Prime Minister Silvio Berlusconi resigned following a vote of no confidence in the Italian parliament and was duly replaced by Mario Monti, another unelected former EU Commissioner.

Having brought Ireland, Greece and Italy to their knees, there are plans for a fiscal compact which will enforce tighter budgetary control, obliging all EU Member States to submit their national budgets for approval and supervision by Brussels, which in effect means Germany, on whose word 'the entire union of 27 countries awaits'.[16] With the exception of the UK, which used its veto, the other 26 countries of the EU agreed to move towards a new treaty that 'confers new powers to the European Court of Justice for policing balanced budget legislation limiting national debt levels in all eurozone countries, and commits the signatories to quasi-automatic penalties against countries that break the 3% maximum limit on budget deficit, with the European Commission as the referee'.[17]

So far, the populace has not had a say on any of these plans. And when they do, whether through a referendum or on the streets: Will the Irish who fought for their independence at great cost to life and limb forgo it so easily? Will the Italians give up their ability to determine their own taxes? Will the Greeks, who fought Nazi occupation house to house not so long ago, surrender their sovereignty just to stay within the

---

16. Jeffrey Sachs, Director of The Earth Institute, Columbia University, *Guardian*, 17 December 2011.

17. *Guardian*, 17 December 2011.

Euro? And will the French give up their budgetary control? If they take to the streets, will we see German troops deployed in Dublin, Rome, Athens and Paris to quell popular unrest? For this is the inescapable logic of further European political integration and fiscal union.

And it goes beyond Europe:

> 'On a day that saw an escalation in the trade battle between China and the United States and a deepening of the diplomatic rift between Britain and France, Christine Lagarde [head of the International Monetary Fund] issued her strongest warning yet about the health of the global economy and said if the international community failed to co-operate, the risk was "retraction, rising protectionism, isolation".'

She added: 'This is exactly the description of what happened in the 1930s, and what followed is not something we are looking forward to.'[18]

Or will they call the bankers' bluff; opt out of capitalism's stranglehold and refuse to pay the banks their pound of flesh; in a word, default? If they do, they may find that it is not the Armageddon that we are told it will be; Ireland, Italy and Greece will not spontaneously combust. Any ensuing pain and hardship would not just be insignificant compared

---

18. *Guardian*, 16 December 2011.

with the everlasting painful austerity in store for us,[19] but it would remove governments' dependence on the financial markets.[20] In 2001, Argentina defaulted on £94 billion, and the country did not fall apart. Instead, it ended up with fewer speculators and more cooperatives.[21] 'Far from the sky falling in, which was what the IMF and the other proponents of orthodoxy predicted, Argentina's growth averaged 9% a year from 2003 to 2007.'[22] 'Ten years ago this month, Buenos Aires's central plaza was echoing with the sound of residents bashing their saucepans in the street... doing whatever they could to be heard to register their anger against the economic mismanagement of their country,' wrote Vicky Baker in the *Guardian* (14 December 2011):

---

19. 'Statistics from the Greek Ministry of Health show a 40% rise in those taking their own lives between January and May this year compared to the same period in 2010', *Guardian*, 19 December 2011.

20. There are those who argue that millions have their pensions tied up with debt repayments and that a default will annihilate those pensions. I suggest asking those pensioners what they would rather do; condemn their children and grandchildren to decades of indignity, unemployment, low pay and shrinking health and social services, all in return for a pension which is dependent on the vagaries of the stock market, or agree a reduced but dignified pension and give their children and grandchildren a future?

21. Fawzi Ibrahim, Default Now, We've Nothing to Lose but Casino Capitalism, *Morning Star*, 13 July 2010.

22. Larry Elliot, Argentina's Path May be Eurozone's Only Option, *Guardian*, 16 April 2012.

'Argentina [was] forced to default on international debt and devalue its currency… Now, one decade later, the South American country is being hailed as a remarkable success story. The economy appears to be booming, with a real GDP growth of 9.1%. Unemployment is down to a 20-year low.'

Had the default been planned and executed earlier, and not forced on Argentina, the flight of '170 billion dollars (equivalent to the country's total foreign debt)'[23] could have been prevented. Numerous African countries have had debt restructured, reduced or wiped out over past decades. A few capitalists bleated as they got richer slower, but the world did not stop spinning on its axis.

In the economic and political turmoil that is gripping the globe, the last thing on the minds of world leaders is concern for the increasing atmospheric CO_2 concentration, the depletion of the polar ice cap or the acidification of the oceans. Capitalism is on a roller coaster with peaks and troughs, bends and loops of unpredictable severity; and the ride has just begun. Among all the uncertainties, one thing is certain; planet Earth is not safe in capitalist hands.

So, what are you doing about it?

---

23. *Guardian*, 20 December 2011.

The Critical Zone – Capitalism at the Edge of a Vortex

The critical zone theory is a derivative of Marx's theory of the tendency of the rate of profit to fall. It divided the development of capitalism into two phases or zones: the traditional or conventional phase and the critical phase. In the conventional phase, rates of profit are high but falling and capital is in relative abundance. In this phase, the fall in the rate of profit is easily compensated for by an increase in investment, which itself puts pressure on the rate of profit to fall further, and so on until a critical threshold is reached. In the critical phase, the rate of profit is at the critical threshold which, if crossed, would require prohibitively large additional capital investment if profits are to be maintained, let alone improved. In contrast to the former relative abundance of capital, capitalism manifests a general deficiency of capital when it crosses the critical threshold.

The movement of the economy from one zone to the other can be illustrated by its operating map or footprint. The operating map of an economy is a graph of the rate of profit plotted against capital outlay with equal profit (EP) curves superimposed on it. The result is a characteristic curve with a downward trajectory as shown in Figure A1.

Since capital accumulates over time, the characteristic curve may look remarkably similar to a time series of the rate of profit showing how the rate of profit changes over time. This is mainly because of price inflation which tends to hide any capital retraction, especially those that normally accompany an economic downturn. By using constant-price figures for capital

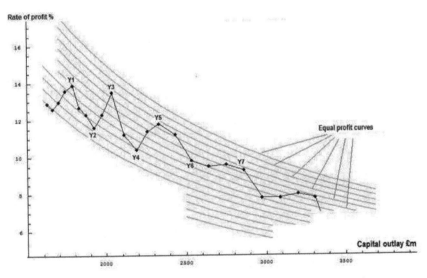

Figure A1 A theoretical economic footprint showing the expected downwards slope as capital accumulates

outlay, capital can be observed in clusters on the operating map where capital retrenchment has occurred.

EMPIRICAL EVIDENCE

The proof that the critical zone theory is valid lies in empirical evidence from a wide range of countries over different timeframes; something that may form a subject for future research. Meanwhile, here are a few examples using readily available data.

The UK economy

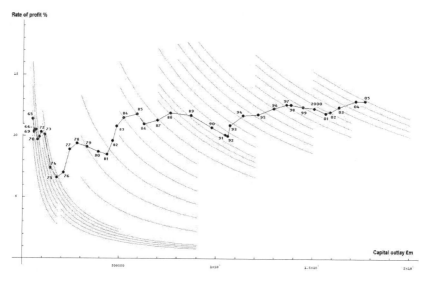

Source: ONS

Figure A2 UK economic footprint for private non-financial corporations, 1965–2005

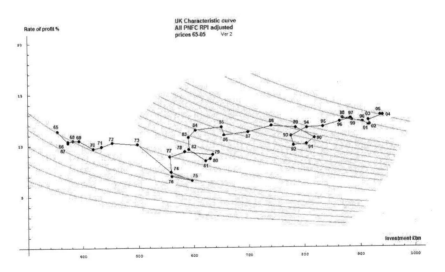

Source: ONS

Figure A3 UK economic footprint for private non-financial corporations, 1965–2005, with RPI-adjusted figures showing capital retrenchment clusters

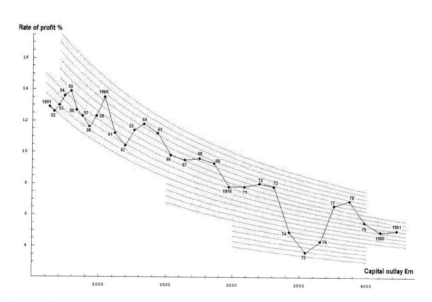

Source: Philip Armstrong, Andrew Glyn and John Harrison, *Capitalism Since World War II*, Fontana, 1984

Figure A4 Economic footprint for UK business, 1951–81

The US economy

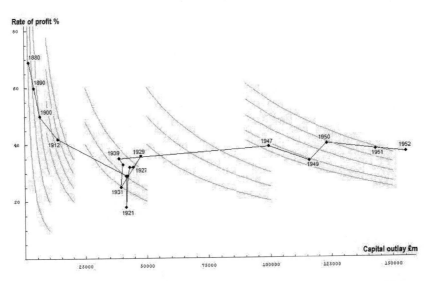

Source: Joseph M Gillman, *The Falling Rate of Profit*, Cameron Associates, 1958

Figure A5 Economic footprint, US manufacturing, 1880–1950

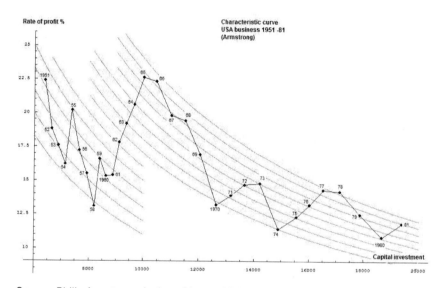

Source: Philip Armstrong, Andrew Glyn and John Harrison, *Capitalism Since World War II*, Fontana, 1984

Figure A6 Economic footprint for US business, 1951–81

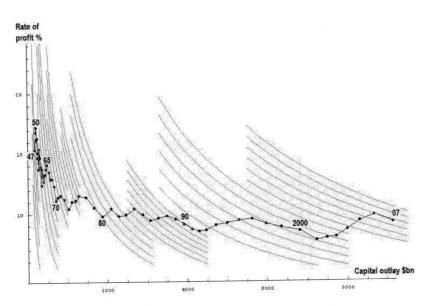

Source: Bureau of Economic Analysis, US Department of Commerce

Figure A7 Economic footprint, US corporations, 1947–2007

Index